Touching the
Far Corners

TOUCHING THE FAR CORNERS

GROWTH IN PRAYER AND MISSION

by Paul Iles

BRITISH AND FOREIGN BIBLE SOCIETY
Stonehill Green, Westlea, Swindon, SN5 7DG, England

A catalogue record for this book is available from the British Library
ISBN 0564 088854

Typeset by BFBS Production Services Department (TP Section)
Printed in Great Britain by Biddles Ltd, Guildford
Cover design by Litchfield Morris, Gloucester
Illustrations by Dominic Harbour

Bible Societies exist to provide resources for Bible distribution and use. The
British and Foreign Bible Society (BFBS) is a member of the United Bible
Societies, an international partnership working in over 180 countries. Their
common aim is to reach all people with the Bible, or some part of it, in a
language they can understand and at a price they can afford. Parts of the Bible
have now been translated into over 2,000 languages. Bible Societies aim to
help every church at every point where it uses the Bible. You are invited to
share in this work by your prayers and gifts. The Bible Society in your
country will be very happy to provide details of its activity.

To my mother

Elizabeth Rosemary

with love and gratitude for her quiet example,

living with joy, trust and perseverance:

life with God – life in prayer

ACKNOWLEDGEMENTS

We are grateful to the following for permission to reproduce copyright material:

Cassells for extracts from *Torrow is Too Late* by Peter Moore;

Christian Action for extracts from *Judge Not* by Eric James;

Darton, Longman and Todd for extracts from *The Dynamic of Tradition* by A.M. Allchin, *Letters from the Desert* by Carlo Carretto, *The True Wilderness* by H.A. Williams and *The Way of Silent Love* by a Carthusian;

Faber and Faber for extracts from *Markings* by Dag Hammarsköld and *Complete Poems and Plays* by T.S. Eliot;

Macmillan and Co. for extracts from *Frequencies* by R.S. Thomas;

Oxford University Press for extracts from *Trevor Huddleston, Essays on his life and work* edited by Deborah Duncan Honore;

Penguin Books for extracts from *Revelations of Divine Love* by Julian of Norwich (edited by Clifton Wolters), *The Fearful Void* by Geoffrey Moorhouse, *The Young Thomas Hardy* by Robert Gittings and *A Time of Gifts* by Patrick Leigh Fermor;

SCM Press for extracts from *Christian Faith and Life* by William Temple;

SPCK for extracts from *Were You There?* by Rosemary Hartill, *The Wisdom of the Derset* by Thomas Merton, *One Light for One World* by Robert Runcie, *Retreat Addresses* by E.K. Talbot and *Life and Fire of Love* by Herbert Waddams;

World Council of Churches for extracts from *Weep Not for Me* by John V. Taylor.

CONTENTS

Preface: using this book   i

Introduction   vii

1   Journey to the sun
    Movement
    Dag Hammarskjöld and Abraham   1

2   Love without measure
    Praise
    Dorothy L. Sayers and Mary   21

3   The fearful void
    Emptiness
    Trevor Huddleston and Elijah   41

4   God of all the nations
    Acceptance
    Mother Teresa and Ruth   60

5   Candle in the wind
    Affliction
    Alexander Solzhenitsyn and Jeremiah   80

6   An exploding heart
    Action
    Brother Roger of Taizé and Andrew   101

Bibliography   120

PREFACE:
USING THIS BOOK

"Why" said the Dodo, "the best way to explain it is to do it."

Lewis Carroll, *Alice in Wonderland*, The Caucus Race

The title of this book comes from a conversation between the actress Patricia Hodge and Sue Lawley in her radio programme *Desert Island Discs*. Patricia Hodge explained that when her first child was born, which was comparatively late in life, she was both prepared and yet unprepared for the birth, and all that followed as her child began to grow. She had certainly wanted a child and yet, she said, giving him birth made her touch the far corners of her being. She found out things about herself which she could never have known before.

When I heard her words I thought of prayer because praying can be like that. The coming of God's Kingdom within his creation is described in the Bible as like the pain of child-bearing. Anyone who prays "thy Kingdom come" will touch many things they have not encountered before.

These studies of contemporary Christians coupled with people from the Bible are not intended to provide another book about prayer but to offer a collection of resource material which, it is hoped, will trigger those who want to pray to explore further afield for themselves in their praying. The material does not attempt to be comprehensive or structured as a course in prayer, although the chapters taken as a whole will offer some sort of shape. Much is left out, but hopefully sufficient help is given for a substantial bit of hiking if not the long march.

In each chapter there is:

- an introduction which aims to outline from two or three slightly different starting points one particular aspect of prayer that every disciple will experience at some time or another;

- two short portraits of men and women of faith who will probably already be known to some extent, and who have "been there" as we say. They have been chosen because their discipleship provides an authentic, personal testimony to the purpose and power of praying. The two people in each chapter can be studied in either order. I have placed Christians from our own times first because we may well have a more immediate rapport with them. To get close to the men and women from the Bible needs some research and background information. If you prefer to begin with Bible study, look for insights and perspectives which can help you in understanding how Christians pray today;

- passages for further reading from a wide range of sources which will open up more ideas and ways ahead.

> *Reading, meditation, prayer and contemplation are so inextricably linked together and support each other in such a way that the first two are pointless without the latter two and one rarely reaches the latter without the former.*
>
> A Carthusian, *The Way of Silent Love*, p. 64

The readings I have chosen reveal those to whom I am indebted for my thinking and praying, and I am specially grateful to them;

- some suggestions for prayer; and written prayers which "collect" together and establish the responses we are making to God.

The men and women in these studies each had their own path to travel. From many different points of departure and arrival, they reveal how the gospel is the same from age to age, and how in each generation with a sure hand God draws his people to himself and leads them into his Kingdom.

THE THEMES

Briefly here is a synopsis of the themes of these studies. Dag Hammarskjöld and Abraham were men prepared to be on the move, quite literally, in their search for God. No one comes to God unless he or she is capable of moving and being moved. Such movement often produces praise, in the first instance, because it is like taking off a brake. Movement releases and sets free. Like the capacity to say thank you, which usually needs to be trained and disciplined if it is to develop and become a natural and gracious aspect of our characters, being able to praise God is a spiritual experience which needs to be valued and developed and enjoyed. Those who are truly moved usually find themselves possessed with a sense of joy, wonder and awe. Mary's song *Magnificat* is a pattern for all Christian praise.

Few, though, who are moved by God and begin to respond to him find that he leaves them there. Inevitably the grounding of prayer in actuality and daily life must follow. We find ourselves wrestling with what St Paul identifies as the flesh and the spirit: two aspects of our experience which can rarely if ever be disentangled, and which come into conflict and tension. Many will experience emptiness when the movement to God and the devotion which flows from it runs into the sand. Then, like Trevor Huddleston who had to discover a source of new life in the barrenness of South Africa's evil practice of apartheid, we have to find out if prayer is real or self-delusion, and discover whether it is a powerful and even a political tool for daily use or just a gesture which spins off into uselessness. Elijah knew emptiness in the desert when he went further and faced the possibility that God did not, after all, even exist.

When our prayers are toughened and challenged by biting experiences like these, we can move into yet another and deeper dimension. We learn how to accept whatever God gives: without complacency, but with trust that his will can be creative and more productive than our own. Acceptance is not giving in to an easy option but moving into the area where the human will and God's will become united and harmonized.

Not everyone is called on to carry a burden of affliction like Solzhenitsyn or Jeremiah, but few escape it altogether and all have to "take up a cross" when they deliberately resolve to follow Jesus. Bearing affliction is not the same as endurance, enduring the periods of emptiness and frustration from which the Spirit cannot save us. Rather it is discovering the way in which in the Spirit such endurance is transformed and turned into a way of redemption; both for those who undergo affliction and for those who witness such things.

Finally, with Brother Roger and St Andrew we consider action: the actual action of praying itself, which often seems like a mirage but which, as Jesus so clearly teaches, is in fact part of the power of the Kingdom and one of the activities of divine sovereignty. We need to penetrate into this aspect of prayer and explore it sufficiently so that we know without doubt that, whatever else it is, praying is activity – an up-front activity, as we might say nowadays, even when it takes place in silence and the secret places. Once we grasp the meaning of prayer as action, then it spills over into the continuing activity of compassion and concern, of witness and political involvement, and all the other aspects of what we used to be taught to call Christian action.

These are some of the places visited by the people in these studies. Recalling them will take us to the same places, which were for them growth points in their life with God, and will invite us to know and name them for ourselves. Living through such periods of growth is life in the Spirit which brings many blessings from God.

The famous spiritual guide Baron Friedrich von Hügel was asked by a friend who was suffering considerable pain for some advice about how to pray within it. He wrote back saying his reply was "intended simply as rough material, or approximate suggestions for your own experimenting and hewing into shape". The same applies to these chapters. I have deliberately not drawn the threads together too tightly and tried to leave the spaces wide open. Each person who prays needs good resources, some guidance, but also – far more useful – much freedom. There will be as many ways of developing this material as there are people praying.

To the individual reader

If you choose to use these resources on your own, one suggestion is, always take the trouble to use a notebook while reading through the first three sections of each chapter and jot down the thoughts and comments which come to you. Your notes will provide the gold from which to develop your prayers. Write it all down if you feel like it. You can trace the patterns and discard the wastage later.

Having worked through the basic material at the beginning of each chapter, the passages for further reading could be taken up at the same time but it will almost certainly be better if you use them later. Let time pass. Return to your notes, read them again, and then read through the passages – not all of them at a sitting perhaps, but as many as you wish – and finally let go, settle down to praying.

Here you can afford to be very open to the Spirit with no attempt
to structure your praying. This may sound risky, but there are ways
of making sure you are coming close to God and not just ram-
bling on. Nearly always, however open you are, you will find a
definite pattern emerging in both prayers and in meditation or
contemplation. God moves our hearts and minds in such a way that
we become aware of (a) adoration, (b) penitence, (c) intercession
or supplication, and (d) self-offering or dedication. Prayers without
any of these ingredients will not be worth very much. So at the end
of each chapter there are suggestions for prayer using these four
headings. Often the shape and order will vary, and rarely will
you find yourself spending the same amount of time on each
subdivision. When you need to draw your prayers to a conclusion,
there are some printed prayers which may help.

To prayer-partners

Individuals find their praying is greatly enriched periodically by
meeting with a prayer-partner. If you follow this suggestion, then
one prayer-partner could look in detail at one of the people
described in each chapter and the other partner could spend time
going into some detail about the other. Then, when you come
together, you will already each have some 'input' to offer. You
could read the opening sections of the chapter to each other in turn,
and the listener each time could jot down thoughts which come to
mind that he or she would like to share with their partner. The two
of you might also take it in turns to lead prayer together.

To group leaders and groups

This book is user-friendly for any groups who would like to
develop and use it. If, however, a group of Christians come
together for prayer, make sure the group is not too big – single
numbers are best.

By now many church groups have developed a good deal of
experience of studying and praying together, and some have been
meeting for a number of years. Whenever new members join, the
dynamics alter, but such groups should try not to be for ever going
back over basics. Some study booklets these days are somewhat
slight in what they have to offer reasonably experienced groups.

However, in these chapters there may be rather too much material than too little and leaders will need to select it carefully, and either thin it down or spread it out and take time over it. I hope group leaders and those who are asked to organize time in retreat will be able to select their own programmes from the material, knowing their needs and particular starting points.

A sensible amount of preparation by each member is necessary to get the best out of any group meeting. Members need to be familiar with the first three sections of the chapter before they meet together. They should also be encouraged to make notes and bring them to the meeting, which could begin by talking through and sharing the notes. This might take twenty minutes to half an hour. A leader would be most helpful if he or she could listen and prepare a framework for praying from the conversation.

For instance, write down any new themes as they emerge, and any words or phrases from Scripture which hold you close to God. Write down any insights which seem particularly fresh and new. Write down the topics about which people are concerned and the names of those for whom they wish to pray. The two middle sections of the chapter about people at prayer could be read aloud. Then have a short break before the time of prayer begins, which might well last another half an hour or so and perhaps include one of the readings.

Praying needs to have both a clear beginning and a definite ending, but it also needs genuine openness in between so that the Spirit can breathe his life into us. It can be useful to place something visual in front of the group – a lighted candle, an open copy of the Bible, an icon, a rosary, a small wooden cross, a bowl of water, these are some suggestions. Music surrounding praying can be useful too; and with cassettes available it is very easy to organize and include it. Time for silence is equally important.

I should like to thank Dominic Harbour for the illustrations which bring the people in this book visually to mind and stimulate the imagination. My thanks to Carol Franklin who prepared the type-script and read the proofs; she also made several helpful suggestions which I was glad to take up. Most of all, my thanks to Simon Reynolds, who not only gave me the original suggestion for this book, but also saw it through to publication.

Paul Iles
Hereford, Easter 1995

INTRODUCTION

*Continue in your faith, firm on your foundations, never to
be dislodged from the hope offered in the gospel which you
heard.*

Colossians 1.21

I try to resist definitions of prayer unless they are simple and direct,
and left as open as possible for further definition. "Prayer is keeping
company with God" was Clement of Alexandria's definition of
prayer at the end of the second century, and I find it exactly right. All
I would add is that the actual activity of praying expresses and
articulates the day-to-day living relationship between God and all
those he creates in his image and likeness. Therefore it cannot but be
a changing experience as all the other relationships we live with have
to be. "New every morning is the love" and each day's prayers are
unique as well.

It is virtually impossible to begin praying starting from scratch.
There will nearly always be something we have already been doing,
perhaps not very well and maybe without calling it prayer, but it
is there and this is what is God-given. Therefore we should never
undervalue it. However threadbare we feel our praying to be, we
should have the confidence to claim it and use it as a beginning: it is
the Spirit within who already is drawing us nearer to God.

So at whatever stage in our prayer-life we think we are, from time
to time it is a good exercise to think through the aspects of praying
with which we are already familiar. Already we want to pray.
Already we feel we cannot pray. Already we have prayed with other
Christians. Already we know some or many disappointments and
heart-break in praying. Already we have some experience of being
with God in Jesus, whether it is through the sacrament of Holy
Communion or through our reading of the Bible, however occasional
attendance and reading has become. Already we have begun to lose
the hard grip on words and started to explore the spaces and feelings
of longing and silence. Already conscience will have warned us that
empty rituals cost nothing and achieve nothing. Don't take any of
this for granted. Use it to the full and turn it into a thank-you prayer
for all that God gives. Thanksgiving remains the primary ground for
growth in the experience of praying.

When we stop and consider our prayers in such a way, we nearly always feel hesitant and uncertain, wondering whether we will ever really begin to pray adequately. But that is another seed of growth. Bishop Michael Ramsey frequently reminded people that "wanting to pray *is prayer*" – or at least a very valid part of it. Prayer is always for beginners and turns those who think they have made progress back into beginners again. Even after a lifetime of growing this is how it remains. One of the desert fathers, Abbot Pambo, as he approached death, remarked, "I go to the Lord as one who has not even made a beginning in the service of God".

We can and should expect praying to be a source of blessing and fruitfulness. Jesus told us, "My yoke is easy and my burden is light" (Matthew 11.30). He was referring to discipleship, but that includes the prayers of those who follow. Prayer really is water in the desert, refreshing and meeting an overwhelming need. It requires discipline and faithfulness, and it will be costly and painful much of the time, but only occasionally should it be something we struggle to do. Praying should not be stressful or create anxiety. If it becomes in any way a source of discomfort or worry, then track back and ask yourself where it has been going wrong.

Praying is never a solo activity even when it is private. A central conviction for growth in prayer is the knowledge that Jesus is always praying with us. He is "the one who ever lives, making intercession" for us (Hebrews 7.25). All who pray belong to a great company of faithful people who want others to join them.

Other people are a vital part of our praying in at least three ways. The first is encouragement: which is a great ingredient in prayer. By talking with one another about prayer and by praying together, we give ourselves a chance to uncover and appreciate it more; like the person who catches their breath suddenly and immediately realizes what it is that keeps them alive. The people who will be with us in these studies are there to support us and by their example to help us to grow, however wide of their mark we may be.

The second is during a time of reflection – *after praying* – when critical reflection and guidance can be very valuable, if not imperative. This too is when discussions with others and reading books is useful. It helps us to make a careful evaluation of our praying – whether we are missing opportunities, whether we are getting things out of proportion, whether we are making a rod for our back instead of finding the joy and rest in the Lord which is promised to those who pray. Remember, though, there is little use in talking about prayer until it is a reality. Discussing theory is unhelpful, while discussing experience stands a chance.

Then third, because the insights we have and any reflections we make on our relationship with God are entirely personal and limited, and they can only be one point of view, genuinely we *need* others to complement and complete what we cannot know and what we do not yet know. They will be able to fill up what we lack. In turn they will need us too, because we shall be able to offer them some experiences of praying which only we know.

Those attempting to explore praying should listen carefully and persistently to one another, and discover how the stages of development in the life of prayer and growth in praying are unpredictable and interchangeable. "The child is father to the man" is partly what this means; but also it means there is no set sequence of growth points through which everyone has to pass in the same order. Growth in prayer is not about jumping a series of hurdles or imitating other people. Instead there are precious insights which those who pray can share. Seek the help of a guide, or what some have called a soulfriend, is and always has been basic advice for those who want to grow through prayer.

"OH, I'VE JUST THROWN ONE OF THOSE AWAY!"

Now spend time identifying what it is you are doing which is already prayer. Ask God to help you value it, to be thankful for it, and do not discard it too soon. Recall:

- the times of inner discovery when you become aware of the context of your life – how you belong to other people – how you know yourself better through other people – how you belong to God – how you can only know yourself fully through knowing God;

- the times when you are moved to hope – or when you are moved to shame and fear, or disappointment – or when you rejoice with others and share in happiness – or when you long for something better and feel incomplete;

- the times when other people's needs are both demanding and overwhelming – think first of people within your own family and among your own friends – then think of the catalogue of human need which the news media presents to us day after day – think of your frailty and powerlessness to help, or do more than scratch the surface – think of the times of suffering and grief you have gone through;

- then think of how you handle these moments – how you have recalled words from the Bible, and from hymns and prayers you know by heart – or how you have recalled your faith in God's goodness and questioned it or wondered if it can be true – think of those who have encouraged you and stood by you, and made you grateful and more confident – think of those whose own personal stories have inspired you and been an example – think of those who have rightly criticized you and helped you to see yourself as others see you, "in your true colours" for better and for worse;

- how often you have read the Bible and tried to say prayers – think of the moments of worship when you have been given new vision – think of the promises and resolutions you have made, even the ones which have been broken and remain unfulfilled – think of the times when God has taken all your concerns out of your hands and held them in his;

- times of stillness and silence when you have glimpsed what it means to be at peace with God, at peace with other people, at peace with yourself – ask yourself whether you need to be alone for such occasions to happen – would being with others at the time hinder or enrich it?

From these thoughts try to build up a vocabulary which sketches out the meaning prayer already has for you.

- What makes you stronger and more able to cope – what releases you from stress and anxiety – what reveals truth to you in such a way that you can handle it, and turn it into something positive rather than negative – what brings you peace of mind, hope and joy – where there is God-given strength and where there is weakness – what is creative within you and how it is overcoming what is destructive.

The words or phrases might be:

- trust – security – forgiveness – confession – penitence – healing – humility – confidence in God rather than self – losing in order to find – renewal or rebirth – serenity – kingdom – cross and resurrection – joy.

There are many steps in prayer and if you have already taken some of them to a greater extent than you imagined or expected, then perhaps what is lacking is an awareness of how these things hold together and strengthen our relationship with God. Many teachers of prayer in our own time have said what we need is to unify and to simplify: to bring things together into a harmonious whole, and to reduce the clutter and baggage so that we can see better what is actually going on through it all. Another step to take might well be to enlarge your concept of praying so that it becomes inclusive instead of exclusive. Usually we are far too narrow and reject too much in our prayers. Then our attempts are built on sand instead of on the rock which is there but is going unnoticed and being unused. Praying includes everything that enables us to relate to God and which sustains and nourishes the relationship.

"ONE OF JESUS' DISCIPLES SAID, 'LORD, TEACH US TO PRAY'" (Luke 11.1)

There is a constant request for more teaching about prayer. Translated, this means at least two things: (a) once start praying and the experience reveals a hunger within which is insatiable in this world and requires constant development; and (b) the actual experience of praying points to a need for growth, movement, and variety, which simply reflects the passage of time within human life. We cannot respond to others, or to God, or even to self in the same way throughout our lives. There is always more to discover.

> *Our prayer has had a beginning because we have had a beginning. But it will have no end. It will accompany us into eternity and will be completed in our contemplation of God.*

> Carlo Carretto, *Letters from the Desert*, p. 35

Praying therefore is totally open and unstructured at one end of its spectrum. Yet most human beings are in some way or another "taught" to pray, and they often receive their first experiences of praying by praying together with others, whether it is sharing the experience with parents, with brothers and sisters, or in school, either Sunday school or school assembly, or in church among the community of those who believe they have been called by God to serve him and love him, or in a smaller group of people who are trying to pray. Praying develops to include this full range of experience: from complete and unstructured openness to the corporate prayers which are treasured and which have been used in many centuries and handed on in the Christian heritage.

Growth implies movement – but not necessarily constant or steady movement. Growth is not to be confused with progress. Within prayer there is probably no place for progress anyway. Instead there are periods of opening up and withdrawal and collapse. There is the desert and Galilee, cross and resurrection, loss and renewal. There is room in prayer for complete freedom of response: we need it and God provides it.

> *Where thou leadest I would go,*
> *Walking in thy steps below,*
> *Till before my Father's throne*
> *I shall know as I am known.*

WHEN?

St Paul says we should pray without ceasing, which means our whole life and every activity within it should be an expression of our relationship with God. But we cannot reach anything like that point without specific times of prayer when we remember and respond to the love and care which God gives us day by day. Specific times of prayer might be:

- worship on the first day of the week to celebrate Jesus' resurrection – the Sunday Eucharist;

- daily prayers – whether twice a day, the traditional morning and evening prayers;

- or three times a day which includes midday;

- or occasionally even "seven times a day", like the monastic offices;

- a discipline chosen by yourself – such as attendance at a weekday Eucharist or a prayer group, perhaps in the evening;

- using arrow prayers at any time;

- any moments deliberately recalling God's presence with us.

A wise friend of mine said, "Usually we give up just at the point when we should press on". This applies whether it's learning the piano or gardening, and you can apply it to hundreds of examples including praying. We must include in our desire for prayer the intention to persist and keep going over a definite period of weeks, long enough to discover the variety and richness within prayer. A useful method of self-help is to work out schemes of prayer which last for a week, or a fortnight, or a month, and vary them as your mood alters and your need changes.

HOW?

Personal decisions and choices again.

1. Find times in the week and in the day which you can spend in prayer – time when you are alert rather than tired. This usually requires quite a careful analysis of your timetable and personal habits. However well you have chosen, though, there are still bound to be times when tiredness robs you of your good intentions; don't be discouraged when this happens or feel you have failed, such times are part of the cycle of living, and can be welcomed and accepted without regret or blame.

2. Make sure you are ready to change or alter the choices you have made. Sometimes you can give more time to praying, sometimes less. Variety is the spice of life and it is one of the best aids to prayer.

3. Remember the advice given when anyone is learning a new language: "a little and often is better than infrequent sessions which are too long and self-defeating". The same with prayer – brevity is a positive virtue – trust the Spirit and allow yourself to be guided when you need to extend and lengthen prayer.

4. Using prayer cards can be very helpful, partly because they contain short prayers which can be said at any time, anywhere, and partly because they can be changed and varied so easily.

WHERE?

Find a place for prayer where above all you can be comfortable and self-forgetful – this includes a good posture for prayer, sitting, kneeling, standing, which again can be varied at any time – and it should almost certainly include a focus for attention like a candle, a cross, or an icon.

Remember, praying rarely brings the same kind of experience, endlessly repeated – there are dry patches as well as "green pastures" – times when the light does not shine as well as times when there is "glory all around". It's worth sometimes changing the room in which you pray, or the place in the room – sometimes face the window, sometimes look into the room itself. These changes often release us and make things fresh.

CALLED TO BE LIVING WITNESSES TO THE MYSTERY OF CHRIST'S CHARACTER (Bishop Hensley Henson)

Was there any development and growth in Jesus' understanding of his Father and in his own prayers and relationship with God? When Jesus says "I and the Father are one" it sounds very static, but it must have been a dynamic relationship in which confidence and trust and hope were unchanging – though often threatened – but within which there was continuing movement and growth.

Although we always have to be reticent and reverent before the mystery of Christ's character, and although we cannot probe Jesus' own consciousness, we can observe aspects of it. A prime example was Gethsemane. We have often heard it described as the moment of supreme testing of Jesus' will, but William Temple in a marvellous passage describes it as also a supreme time of inward growth.

> *"'Let there be light'; and there was light." "And he was parted from them about a stone's cast; and he kneeled down and prayed, saying, Father, if thou be willing, remove this cup from me; nevertheless not my will, but thine be done... And being in an agony he prayed more earnestly; and his sweat was, as it were, great drops of blood falling down upon the ground."*

*In those two quotations there is depicted the difference for
God between creating the universe with its millions of
stars, and the making of a selfish soul into a loving one. To
create was easy; the will of God produces its own
fulfilment; no effort there. "'Let there be light'; and there
was light." But to convert hearts like our hearts from the
self-centredness which is natural to them into the love which
is God's own nature, which they must reach if they are to be
in fellowship with him – that costs the agony and the bloody
sweat and the death upon the Cross.*

William Temple, *Christian Faith and Life*

Such an experience points us towards the goal of our own growth
in praying, which is maturity, "measured by nothing less than the
full stature of Christ" (Ephesians 4.13). Jesus has promised to pray
with us while this is happening and he will enable us to handle and
bring into play at least some of these:

• times of success and failure;

• reason and emotion;

• humility and poverty of Spirit;

• rejection and misunderstanding;

• confidence and victory in the Spirit;

• an ability to see deep down into things and accept them;

• the ability to recognize where true strength lies and build on it.

FOR MEDITATION

1. Exhortation to prayer

> *What various hindrances we meet*
> *In coming to a mercy-seat!*
> *Yet who that knows the worth of pray'r*
> *But wishes to be often there?*
>
> *Pray'r makes the dark'ned cloud withdraw,*
> *Pray'r climbs the ladder Jacob saw,*
> *Gives exercise to faith and love,*
> *Brings ev'ry blessing from above.*

> *Restraining pray'r, we cease to fight;*
> *Pray'r makes the Christian's armour bright;*
> *And Satan trembles, when he sees*
> *The weakest saint upon his knees.*
>
> *While Moses stood with arms spread wide,*
> *Success was found on Israel's side;*
> *But when thro' weariness they fail'd,*
> *That moment Amalek prevail'd.*
>
> *Have you no words? Ah, think again!*
> *Words flow apace when you complain*
> *And fill your fellow-creature's ear*
> *With the sad tale of all your care.*
>
> *Were half the breath thus vainly spent*
> *To heav'n in supplication sent,*
> *Your cheerful song would oft'ner be:*
> *"Hear what the Lord has done for me!"*

William Cowper

2. Growth in the Spirit

It is dangerous for any Christian to think that for spiritual progress his prayer is necessarily bound to go through a fixed series of manoeuvres. The best analogy is that of growth. Prayer is growth in the love of God. In every person the capabilities of growth are different, the hindrances to growth vary, the speed of growth is not the same. In some plants the flowers come before the leaves, in others there is little stem, while in yet others there are no flowers at all except perhaps for one day before the plant dies. So it is with the human soul.

Herbert M. Waddams, *Life and Fire of Love*

3. Christian formation

At its heart, the wellspring of our life is divine love, and the goal of our lives is divine love; and the way into which formation seeks to move us can be nothing other than divine love, that is to say, the love of God poured out in our hearts by the Holy Spirit who dwells in us (Romans 5.5). The Spirit alone can search the depths of God, the Spirit alone communicates the life and love of God, the Spirit alone, the anointing that teaches us from within, is able to guide us in the ways of God, to the Father.

A Carthusian, *The Way of Silent Love*

PRAYERS

O Holy Spirit, Giver of light and life, impart to us thoughts higher than our own thoughts, and prayers better than our own prayers, and powers beyond our own powers; that we may spend and be spent in the ways of love and goodness; after the perfect image of our Lord and Saviour Jesus Christ. Amen

Milner White, Daily Prayer

Defend, O Lord, your servant with your heavenly grace, that I may continue yours for ever, and daily increase in your Holy Spirit more and more, until I am brought to your everlasting kingdom. Amen

Adapted from the Confirmation Service

Grant Lord, that we may hold to you without parting, worship you without wearying, serve you without failing; faithfully seek you, happily find you, and for ever possess you, the only God, blessed, now and for ever.   Amen

St Anselm, 1033–1109

1 JOURNEY TO THE SUN
MOVEMENT

INTRODUCTION

Launch out into the deep (Luke 5.4)

I heard Rabbi Lionel Blue telling some of his friends, "It's always better to talk to God than to talk about him". He was quoting a Christian saint, and he went on to suggest everyone should take time for such conversations with God and then, as he said, "see where they take you".

In other words Christians, and indeed those who do not yet claim the name but who are heading in the same direction, are people capable of movement, who actively seek it, and who are always genuinely open to outside influences. He or she is not where they once were and yet still not where they would like to be. They are journeying but not at journey's end. Using an old Latin tag, they are always *in media res*, in the midst of things, and they often have to be prepared to travel forward without exactly knowing the destination, having to accept and trust only the "hints and guesses" which emerge along the way.

Abraham "went out, not knowing where he was to go" (Hebrews 8.11). Such an experience can be exhilarating and exciting, but frankly it can also be confusing, disappointing, and frustrating. The same mixture of emotions come to most of us while praying, and considerable skill and not a little help is needed to handle them if they are not to throw us off balance.

There are two facts to hold on to: one is that God himself is also moving and he can be trusted to be present with us *in the midst* of whichever bit of the mix and muddle we are facing at the time. The other is to remember the place of departure and to recognize what has already happened – to identify what God has *already done for us* (and there is always something), to be thankful for it, to celebrate it, and build on it.

Reflecting on his own turbulent life as a disciple, the hymn writer John Newton (1725–1807) says:

> *I am not what I ought to be,*
> *I am not what I would wish to be,*
> *I am not what I hope to be,*
> *But, by the grace of God, I am not what I was.*

This sounds very like the famous "restlessness" described by St Augustine, being tossed hither and thither by ourselves and by God until we achieve our destiny. Whether such constant movement develops into grace abounding or destabilizes and debilitates us depends on whether we are living in God as fully as we can, whether we are in touch with our inner life, whether our praying is enabling us to journey on.

One of the turning points in discipleship, when enquiry becomes belief, is when we know and accept that movement of this kind is a foundation of all Christian spirituality, not an optional extra for some rather than for all. Moving towards God and moving with him is a way of making the leap of faith and being a follower of Jesus.

Is there anybody there?

We have already said that prayer is everything which establishes and articulates our relationship with God. Yet our praying often threatens to collapse into a monologue and become self-indulgence. Many times in praying we discipline ourselves to keep silent and not do all the talking. But, equally, there are times when we can expect God to listen and allow us to talk. He wants to hear. He is the one who listens. In his praying, Abraham often talks and argues with God (for example read Genesis 17.18–33). God creates us for a lively partnership with him which is full-blooded and meaningful, rather than pale, abject, and limp. C. S. Lewis once wrote that our desires are usually too weak for God rather than too strong. Prayer can feel hollow and unfulfilled unless there is a developing understanding of how this particular kind of "dialogue" works, which is unlike the conversations in which we usually take part.

Cynics easily ridicule prayer and say it's talking to ourselves or into thin air. But such criticism can be worked through, and those who talk with God rather than about him will experience prayer which is not posturing or an empty gesture but is a fulfilling relationship.

Master, they say that when I seem
To be in speech with you,
Since you make no replies, it's all a dream
– One talker aping two.

They are half right, but not as they
Imagine; rather, I
Seek in myself the things I meant to say,
And lo! the wells are dry.

Then, seeing me empty, you forsake
The Listener's role, and through
My dead lips breathe and into utterance wake
The thoughts I never knew.

And thus you neither need reply
Nor can; thus, while we seem
Two talking, thou art One forever, and I
No dreamer, but they dream.

C. S. Lewis

Think of the many forms listening to God and hearing him can take. Word and Sacrament has been the traditional way of describing them and each of the following fits into these categories:

- Scripture is God's word;

- the actual presence of Christ among his people, known in the breaking of bread and in the neighbour who every day speaks a contemporary "Word of God";

- those who are our companions in the faith, from past and present; they will regularly be used by God to speak with us; hearing them and their testimonies are more "words from God";

- God also speaks through his whole creation – people with their achievements and needs, the beauty of the natural world, the events of history.

There may be other ways you can think of – they all provide the raw material within which those with ears to hear can listen to God and enjoy a genuine dialogue with him. Praying is wide and flexible enough to include them all when it is a full partnership with God and not the dull echo of self.

In him we live and move and have our being (Acts 17.28)

Prayer holds together God's initiative in coming to us with what Michel Quoist called the Christian response and makes them a single experience. Prayer is the creative movement from God to us and back again. St Augustine described how, at some point in this mutuality, every Christian comes to understand that we cannot rightly speak of finding God without acknowledging that this must include being found by him; nor of wanting to know God without implying that he too wants to know us and to be known by us. There are not two separate experiences which dove-tail, but two aspects of the same experience.

We need an unusual kind of perception to recognize and understand the mutuality in the relationship between God and ourselves which praying claims to create. Not many have properly analysed or described it, perhaps because it seems to set human beings and the divine on such an equal footing that it can look like irreverence and pride. It could be both. But if we remember that any mutuality there is between creature and Creator is of God's choosing, then we can investigate it and experience it eagerly, incautiously, and without fear.

It might be easier to say of desire, longing, knowing, loving that each has a double dimension involving both God and ourselves. Probably this is what some have meant when they tell us God is closer to us than breathing – something we can hardly separate from ourselves even to identify and describe. And it is this same double perspective which frees us from the wrong kind of anxiety which tempts us to dismiss the religious life as delusion and self-deception. Again, once we start talking with God instead of about him then we experience this mutuality and it holds us in being.

We often describe experiencing God's desire for our friendship and love as being "called by God". Both Dag Hammarskjöld, our contemporary, and Abraham, from the ancient world, illustrate in their own very different ways what the call of God means. Their stories are how they became aware of God and responded to him. Yet, however much we open ourselves to the growing unity of Spirit between God and ourselves, we shall still often feel there is a great gulf fixed at the heart of the experience which creates division and separation between the partners, or, in twentieth-century language, a feeling of alienation. Dag Hammarskjöld and Abraham had deep shadows at the centre of their faith. Neither could easily understand or explain what God was asking of them. But somehow in the coming of God to us, and the approach of human beings to God there is costly movement in both partners which is part of the same journey.

If the purpose of all this movement, growth, development, and change within any person is that he or she may know and be known by God, then think of this: when through our praying our relationship with God is as deep and as intimate as we have described it, there will also be the same movement, growth, development, and change taking place within God himself. For he encompasses and takes to himself the whole relationship which his loving establishes with us. If we live in him and he lives in us then he cannot but be dynamic and moving.

I realize how many assumptions I am making in talking of God like this and I recognize that I have strongly tended towards an old-fashioned way of speaking – anthropomorphism – which is impossible for many people nowadays.

Jay, a character in A. N. Wilson's novel *The Vicar of Sorrows*, says to Francis Kreer the priest, "I do meditate, even though I can't pray exactly. No one has ever taught me how to pray. I do not know who I'd be praying to." Somehow we need to get beyond that opaque state.

Like many others, I ruled out the old man in the skies long ago, but I have not stopped believing that God is personal, dynamic, and purposeful. In the relationship we experience through praying these are the divine characteristics which are at work in us and also at work in the world itself. We need acceptable ways to picture and describe our relationship with God which contain these attributes. Even acknowledging the impossibility of finding adequate words to use, our language is too thin, too vague; mistakes which we confuse with reverence and humility. One reason why our praying may be weaker than it need be is our inability to find ways of talking about God which include divine energy, activity, and desire.

Such thoughts appear to contradict the more usual picture of God as unchanging and immovable, and there may be times when we need to return to the classic thought about God, but there are many more times I suspect when God gives himself more dangerously into our hands and allows himself to be vulnerable to our misunderstanding and mistreatment.

We often say we see into the heart of God through the death and resurrection of Jesus. There God is utterly careless of his own self-protection. When we look at the lives of Dag Hammarskjöld and

Abraham we can see how few movements and journeys of faith
have no hazards or dangers. Living in the Spirit is never without
risks. To be in the Spirit is an adventure because it is a sign of
being fully alive and being truly loving. Movement both in God
and in ourselves is a sign of vitality and love in each partner, a sign
of how much God lives for us and loves us, and how much we live
for him and respond with our love.

DAG HAMMARSKJÖLD

A dictionary of biography describes Dag Hammarskjöld:

> Dag Hammarskjöld (1905–61) *Swedish administrator and
> (from 1953) secretary general of the United Nations. He
> was the son of a Conservative prime minister of Sweden
> and had served his country in general administrative posts
> before succeeding Trygve Lie at the United Nations (UN).
> He did much to extend the executive powers of the
> secretariat, especially by his organization and utilization of
> UN forces in the Congo (1961). While flying to Ndola in
> what was then Northern Rhodesia on a truce-making
> mission, he was killed in an air crash. He was
> posthumously awarded the Nobel Peace Prize.*

After Dag Hammarskjöld's death a manuscript was found beside
his bed in his apartment on East 73rd Street in New York. It
contained jottings of a spiritual diary kept for over 31 years,
written for no eyes but his own. When they were published with
the title *Markings*, they came as an enormous surprise. Nearly
everyone had taken this international diplomat, this reserved man,
who very seldom went to church and who drove himself hard with
a will of steel, to be an agnostic humanist dedicated to the service
of humankind. But he had himself lived through "a wilderness
experience" both on the world stage and in his own inner life.

His family had lived in the splendour of a sixteenth-century
castle at Uppsala, Sweden, a university city, where he was born.
His ancestors on his father's side had been chiefly soldiers and
politicians; and on his mother's, clergy and scholars. His mother
had a deep influence on him. He was brought up as a rather liberal
Lutheran. At the university his faith was eroded. This kind of
scepticism is no modern thing and has been with us for
generations. Dag Hammarskjöld did well as a student. He also

became a connoisseur of art and a keen mountaineer. Soon after leaving university he went into finance and government service. His future looked "made". Then he was elected secretary general of the UN and, significantly for his own personal search, he said the challenge of this key post was "the greatest of blessings as well as the greatest of burdens".

For eight years he lived a well-packed life – working at his always tidy desk with seldom more than a couple of papers on it, making difficult decisions, facing tough men like Kruschev, travelling the world. "He was a man of quiet but incredible energy", a colleague said, "I have never worked with anyone who seemed so impervious to fatigue". People often say: "If you live at this kind of pressure, it will steam-roller your religion out of you", but with Dag Hammarskjöld it did precisely the opposite. It was within the most extreme pressure that his life of prayer really grew. He was rather like the man who said, "When I get up I always pray for at least a few minutes, but if I know I am going to be really busy, I pray for nearly an hour".

Dag Hammarskjöld found that his way to faith – or his way back to faith – was a long journey. If we read his notes and jottings in *Markings*, we can see how for long periods nothing new or illuminating turns up. He could not take over patterns of belief and devotion from others, but had to think them out for himself, wrestling and working at them. "There is no formula to teach us how to arrive at maturity," he wrote, "and there is no grammar of the language of the inner life". He developed an interest in the mystics – not for their spiritual experiences which perhaps he could not share, but because, as he said, "Love for them, was a surplus of power which they felt completely filled them when they began to live in self-forgetfulness". He quoted Psalm 78.35 "they remembered that God was their strength". The whole psalm recalls the experience of the Jews in the wilderness when they forgot God and grew distant from him.

But in spite of a sense of separation from God which is common, for all who still have the courage to make a spiritual pilgrimage there are "moments of disclosure". Sometimes we hardly notice them. Often we remain suspicious of them. We examine them hesitantly or even reluctantly. We never want to be taken in, but we should learn to respect these moments and treat them as precious gifts from God. They usually contain the very secrets we long for, and they build up and nourish our faith.

Here are some moments which Dag Hammarskjöld was able to use on his journey.

> *I am being driven forward*
> *Into an unknown land.*
> *The pass grows steeper,*
> *The air colder and sharper.*
> *A wind from my unknown goal*
> *Stirs the strings*
> *Of expectation.*
>
> *Still the question:*
> *Shall I ever get there?*
> *There where life resounds,*
> *A clear pure note*
> *In the silence.*

1925

I said in my heart to him, I who in sins and doubts and in my grievous separation reach out my hands: reach out thy hand and touch me, O most holy One.

Meditation for Communion

In our era the road to holiness necessarily passes through the world of action.

Markings, 1955

I don't know Who or What put the question. I don't know when it was put. I don't even remember answering. But at some moment I did answer Yes to Someone – or Something – and from that hour I was certain that existence is meaningful, and that, therefore, my life, in self-surrender, had a goal.

From that moment I have known what it means "not to look back", and "to take no thought for the morrow".

Led by the Ariadne's thread of my answer through the labyrinth of Life, I came to a time and place where I realised that the Way leads to a triumph which is a catastrophe, and to a catastrophe which is a triumph, that the price for committing one's life would be reproach, and that the only elevation possible to man lies in the depths of humiliation. After that, the word "courage" lost its meaning, since nothing could be taken from me.

As I continued along the Way, I learned, step by step, word by word, that behind every saying in the Gospels, stands one *man and* one *man's experience. Also behind the prayer that the cup might pass from him and his promise to drink it. Also behind each of the words from the Cross.*

Markings, Whitsunday, 1961

Dag Hammarskjöld spoke to God in the secret places of his heart and writings, although in public he rarely if ever spoke about him. Clearly such a way of life is costly, demanding a total offering of self within the constant activities and anxieties of ordinary everyday life. But he found that to live with a vocation and to make life a pilgrimage is a response to God in our own century with the same integrity as it had for Abraham, and for so many others in every culture and age.

ABRAHAM

Abraham was the father of the patriarchs; a hero whose spiritual life showed great trust in the demands of God, especially on two occasions – when he was asked to go out into an unknown country and when he was asked to give back to God his own son, not knowing for certain what would be the outcome. He was called "the friend of God", one with whom God spoke directly, face to face, and who "told him everything"; one who spoke *with* God rather than *about* him.

Although the account of Abraham's life is set out in detail in Genesis, we start instead with two other passages in the Old Testament which were written at different periods of history, but which both show how Abraham was regarded by the Jewish people.

Joshua 24.2–4

The first passage provides a useful summary of the stories in the second part of Genesis (from chapter 12 onwards) which tell the details of Abraham's life and adventures.

> *Joshua said to all the people, "Thus says the Lord the God*
> *of Israel, 'Your fathers lived of old beyond the Euphrates,*
> *Terah, the father of Abraham and of Nahor; and they*
> *served other gods. Then I took your father Abraham from*
> *beyond the River and led him through all the land of*
> *Canaan, and made his offspring many. I gave him Isaac;*
> *and to Isaac I gave Jacob and Esau. And I gave Esau the*
> *hill country of Seir to possess, but Jacob and his children*
> *went down to Egypt.'"*

It's worth reading the whole passage some time (Joshua 24.1–18) because it sets out briefly the history of the origins of the Jewish people and puts it in a religious context. The Jews believed that because God had chosen, guided, and protected their ancestors, they were committed to him in a unique way because he had committed himself to them. In the Bible, historical events and religious understanding go hand in hand. Can we recover this insight and see God at work in history today?

Isaiah 41.8–10

The second passage comes from a much later period of Jewish history, written while the Jews were in exile, so it reflects a second "wilderness experience", when they lacked the strength and devotion of a settled religious life "at home", and when their confidence in God was again being tested to the limit.

The writer continues to look back beyond the Exodus to the story of Abraham, which he takes to be the beginning of his people's knowledge of God's love. God had promised to protect them always, and now in such terrible circumstances they need to remember that he never breaks faith.

> *But you Israel, my servant,*
> *Jacob, whom I have chosen,*
> *the offspring of Abraham, my friend;*
> *you whom I took from the ends of the earth,*
> *and called you from its farthest corners,*
> *saying to you, "You are my servant",*
> *I have chosen you and not cast you off;*
> *fear not, for I am with you, be not dismayed, for I am your*
> *   God; I will strengthen you, I will help you, I will uphold*
> *   you with my victorious right hand.*

Abraham, like Dag Hammarskjöld, brings before us at least two themes which we can turn into prayer:

1. the adventure of responding to God's call;

2. the covenant or promise made between God and those he calls, which can be trusted and relied on at all times and in all places, no matter what circumstances surround us.

READINGS

1. Pilgrimages

> *There is an island there is no going*
> *to but in a small boat the way*
> *the saints went, travelling the gallery*
> *of the frightened faces of*
> *the long-drowned, munching the gravel*
> *of its beaches. So I have gone*
> *up the salt lane to the building*
> *with the stone altar and the candles*
> *gone out, and kneeled and lifted*
> *my eyes to the furious gargoyle*
> *of the owl that is like a god*
> *gone small and resentful. There*
> *is no body in the stained window*
> *of the sky now. Am I too late?*
> *Were they too late also, those*
> *first pilgrims? He is such a fast*
> *God, always before us and*
> *leaving as we arrive.*

R. S. Thomas, *Pilgrimages*

2. Towards the East

"A splendid afternoon to set out!", said one of the friends who was seeing me off, peering at the rain and rolling up the window.

The other two agreed. Sheltering under Curzon Street arch of Shepherd Market, we had found a taxi at last. In Half Moon Street, all collars were up. A thousand glistening umbrellas were tilted over a thousand bowler hats in Piccadilly; the Jermyn Street shops, distorted by streaming water, had become a submarine arcade; and the clubmen of Pall Mall, with china tea and anchovy toast in mind, were scuttling for sanctuary up the steps of their clubs. Blown askew, the Trafalgar Square fountains twirled like mops, and our taxi, delayed by a horde of Charing Cross commuters reeling and stampeding under a cloudburst, crept into The Strand. The vehicle threaded its way through a flux of traffic. We splashed up Ludgate Hill and the dome of St Paul's sank deeper in its pillared shoulders. The tyres slewed away from the drowning cathedral and a minute later the silhouette of The Monument, descried through veils of rain, seemed so convincingly liquefied out of the perpendicular that the tilting thoroughfare might have been forty fathoms down. The driver as he swerved wetly into Upper Thames Street, leaned back and said: "Nice weather for young ducks."

How strange it seemed – feeling suddenly forlorn; but only for a moment – to be setting off from the heart of London! No beetling cliffs, no Arnoldian crash of pebbles. I might have been leaving for Richmond, or for a supper of shrimps and whitebait at Gravesend, instead of Byzantium.

Patrick Leigh Fermor, *A Time of Gifts*

3. Pilgrims

Throughout the Middle Ages and up to 1500 or thereabouts, the vast majority of those who dragged themselves across the Alps were pilgrims, all with a single objective: the saving of their souls. Their primary goal was almost invariably Rome, where they

*intended to pray at the shrines of both St Peter
and St Paul; but their journey might well include,
for good measure, those of St Matthew at Salerno,
of St Mark in Venice and, quite possibly, of
the Archangel Michael in his deep cave beneath
Monte Gargano on the Adriatic coast.*

*They travelled hard, on horseback and on foot, and
during the two or three years that they might expect to
be on the road they must have had plenty of time to
look about them. But of all the many accounts that they
left behind, few, if any, give more than a cursory mention
of the countryside through which they passed.*

John Julius Norwich, *Landscape with Space for the Soul*

4. The cost of discipleship

*Once when great crowds were accompanying him,
Jesus turned to them and said: "If anyone comes to me
and does not hate his father and mother, wife and
children, brothers and sisters, even his own life, he
cannot be a disciple of mine. No one who does not
carry his cross and come with me can be a disciple of
mine. Would any one of you think of building a
tower without first sitting down and calculating the
cost, to see whether he could afford to finish it?
Otherwise, if he has laid its foundations and then is
not able to complete it, all the onlookers will laugh
at him. 'There is the man', they will say, 'who started
to build and could not finish'. Or what king will
march to battle against another king, without first
sitting down to consider whether with ten thousand
men he can face an enemy coming to meet him with
twenty thousand? If he cannot, then, long before
the enemy approaches, he sends envoys, and asks for
terms. So also none of you can be a disciple of mine
without parting with all his possessions."*

Luke 14.25–33

5. Welcome home

*Now that which caused me to come on pilgrimage was
this: we had one Mr Tell-true come into our parts, and
he told it about what Christian had done, that went from
the City of Destruction – namely, how he had forsaken
his wife and children, and had betaken himself to a
pilgrim's life. It was also confidently reported how he
had killed a serpent that did come out to resist him in his
journey; and how he got through to whither he intended.
It was also told what welcome he had at all his Lord's
lodgings, especially when he came to the gates of the
Celestial City; for there, said the man, he was received
with sound of trumpet by a company of shining ones. He
told, also, how all the bells in the city did ring for joy at
his reception, and what golden garments he was clothed
with; with many other things that now I forbear to relate.
In a word that man so told the story of Christian and his
travels, that my heart fell into a burning haste to be gone
after him; nor could father or mother stay me. So I got
from them, and am come this far on my way.*

John Bunyan, *Pilgrim's Progress*

6. Crowning absurdity

*The peculiar Jewish story [of Abraham] begins at the
end, at the end of a man's life. The man was old,
certain of death, waiting while pretending not to wait.
And at that moment the unreasonable, absurdly
hopeful spirit of life asserted itself. It called him –
perhaps out of a bush set on fire by the setting sun or
the smell of spring. It reminded him of what he had
once wanted to do and had not done. And the foolish
old man left behind him all certainty, all security,
everything he knew, and went he knew not where in
search of he knew not what, because "he-knew-what"
and because he preferred the promise to certainty. He
went – and in his going he became the father of faith.
This going was his faith and in such going the world
becomes promising once more.*

And by this going of an old man in search of a new life here and now and always, so the teller of that tale wants to tempt us into believing, the life of man is turned into a parable, into a poem of absurd promise. Ever after, he insisted with sublime Jewish arrogance, Abraham would be a blessing to anyone who found his folly more promising than the wisdom of the resigned. And unenviable for ever and ever would be the fate of the man who saw nothing very promising in the going of that old man.

Werner Pelz, *Crowning Absurdity*

7. Conversion

"one moment when I bowed my head,
And the whole world turned over
And came upright".

G. K. Chesterton

Ask yourself these questions.

- *Have I ever considered how real God's call can be? Have I ever considered how it came to me?* Each person has his or her own story to tell: a story which may well yet be incomplete. Some have a "conversion experience", some have a slow "learning process", some treasure and value the family they were born into, the Christian communities to which they have belonged, particular people who have "brought them to Christ", some indeed have many adventures along the way, visiting various "far countries" where they cannot find God.

- *Am I able to trust God's promise? Do I have any evidence that "he saves" to use a biblical phrase – rescuing, protecting, guiding, walking with me?* Recall the events which fit these various aspects of living with God. Mark them out in some way, with gratitude. Why is it so hard to trust God's promises? What should we do when he appears to be absent or powerless?

* *What will I be willing to give up if I believe God is asking me to to go through my own wilderness or Gethsemane?* Perhaps out of context this is a false question: perhaps we resist hypothetical questions but instead pray that we may always be ready for the cost to self of every eventuality.

PRAYERS

1. Adoration

In this is love, not that we loved God but that he loved us and sent his Son.

1 John 4.10

Begin by giving thanks for the movement which God is making towards you without which you could not begin to turn to him.

2. Penitence

Jesus once gave a stern warning, "No one who puts his hand to the plough and looks back is fit for the kingdom of God".

Luke 9.62

Ask for forgiveness for times of weakness and lack of resolve which have held you back from moving ahead into God's kingdom.

3. Intercession

At the sheep-pool in Jerusalem there is a place with five colonnades. In these colonnades there lay a crowd of sick people, blind, lame, and paralysed. Among them was a man who had been crippled for thirty-eight years. When Jesus saw him lying there and was aware that he had been ill a long time, he asked him, "Do you want to recover?" "Sir" he replied, "I have no one to put me in the pool when the water is disturbed, but while I am moving, someone else in the pool before me". Jesus answered, "Rise to your feet, take up your bed and walk."

John 5.2–9

Pray for all those who cannot move towards God for whatever reason and ask God to use you, as he used Jesus, to bring healing and new life to others.

4. Dedication

Jesus said, "You did not choose me: but I chose you. I appointed you to go on and bear fruit, fruit that shall last".

John 15.16

Ask God to enable you to give yourself to him so completely that you may work for his kingdom and enjoy its fruitfulness and fulfilment.

5. Written Prayers

Gracious and holy Father, give us wisdom to perceive you, diligence to seek you, patience to wait for you, eyes to behold you, a heart to meditate on you, and a life to proclaim you; through the power of the Spirit of Jesus Christ our Lord. Amen

St Benedict 480–550

Teach us, O God, to walk trustfully each day in your presence, that your voice may encourage us, your arm defend us, and your love surround us; through Jesus Christ our Lord. Amen

Lord God, you call your servants to ventures of which we cannot see the ending, by paths as yet untrodden, through perils unknown; give us faith to go out with good courage, not knowing whither we go, but only that your hand is leading us, and your love supporting us; to the glory of your name.   Amen

2 LOVE WITHOUT MEASURE
PRAISE

INTRODUCTION

Praise the Lord, O my soul: and all that is within me praise his Holy Name (Psalm 103.1)

Songs of Praise remains one of the most popular of all religious programmes on television. One critic described it as 'an oasis of goodness', and perhaps the appeal is more fundamental even than that.

> *The only reason to praise God is not in order to benefit man (though to praise God does in fact benefit him) nor of course to benefit God, but simply because it was for this that man was created. Man is not complete until he glorifies God, in word and in deed. The most sound, the most complete, the most joyful thing that he can do is to praise God.*

> A. M. Allchin, *The Dynamic of Tradition*, p. 91

Our relationship with God is based on praise and often what moves us to speak with God is a simple outpouring of emotion. More basic than prayers of asking are prayers of praise.

> *How good to give thanks to the Lord:*
> *to sing praises to your name O Most High,*
> *to declare your love in the morning:*
> *and at night to sing of your faithfulness.*

> Psalm 92.1–2

In the Bible the proper human response to any awareness of God which we may have is wonder and love, providing a secure foundation for the relationship expressed through praying to grow and develop. Even before God's holiness reveals our personal unworthiness and begins the task of cleansing, the same holiness

reveals God's glory and his amazing grace in opening it to us.
Whenever we are brought face to face with God, there are
moments of genuine ecstasy when we are "taken out of ourselves".

St Basil the Great (c. 330–79) begins his teaching on prayer
like this:

> *Twofold, beloved, are the methods of prayer. One is to give*
> *praise to God from a humble heart; the other, the lower, is*
> *the prayer of petition. Therefore, when you pray, do not*
> *immediately begin with petitions; otherwise you may then*
> *be accused of praying to God only when in need. So when*
> *you come to pray, leave self behind, let the earth go and*
> *rise up to heaven, leave behind every creature, the visible*
> *and the invisible, and begin with the praise and glory of*
> *Him who has made all things.*

Praise is always the priority in praying, and it disciplines and
corrects the unending human tendency to put self first rather than
God. It is very easy to slip into bad habits without noticing, and
allow the tendency to self-centredness to spread, to cling to our
prayers and to cover everything.

In one of her talks, Evelyn Underhill points us firmly in the
right direction:

> *see how persistent, all through the ancient daily offices*
> *from which our Morning and Evening Prayer are drawn,*
> *is the emphasis on God's Being, rather than on man's*
> *needs. The Psalms – the greatest number of which are*
> *poems praising God, exalting his greatness and mercy, his*
> *cherishing care, over against the littleness of men, or*
> *meditating on some aspect of his nature – these are to be*
> *the regular daily food of the worshipping soul.*

Evelyn Underhill, *The Mount of Purification*, p. 196

Give me joy in my heart

C. S. Lewis said among his difficulties with Christianity both before
and after his acceptance of faith was the centrality of praise. He could
not see its purpose in spirituality and worship until he realized:

> *The world rings with praise – lovers praising their*
> *mistresses, readers their favourite poet, walkers praising*
> *the countryside, players praising their favourite game –*

praise of weather, wines, dishes, actors, motors, horses, colleges, countries, historical personages, children, flowers, mountains, rare stamps, rare beetles, even sometimes politicians or scholars. I had not noticed how the humblest, and at the same time most balanced and capacious minds, praised most, while the cranks, misfits and malcontents praised least.

C.S. Lewis, *Reflections on the Psalms*, p. 94

Giving praise to God is a very healthy and creative activity. It leads on to finding all that is worth praising in every aspect of creation, and it helps us to conquer cynicism, discontent, and boredom. The world stops collapsing in on us and opens out instead. Praise releases our powers of imagination and reason, thought and invention.

Give me joy in my heart, keep me praising,
give me joy in my heart, I pray;
give me joy in my heart, keep me praising,
keep me praising till the break of day.

The glory of God is a living person (St Irenaeus, c. 130–200)

Praise is a source of depth and growth in the Spirit. But beyond the moments of inspiration how is it produced? The poetry of Psalm 92 couples together praise and thanksgiving, suggesting we should look for things for which we can be thankful. The old recipe of counting blessings is not as out of date as it sounds. I find this passage quoted by Canon Allchin in his book *A Taste of Liberty* very moving. The Welsh writer D.J. Williams in his autobiography is describing his mother:

Very often when she was busy at her work, without dreaming that anyone was listening, I would hear her chanting her prayers and meditations, in a quiet adoring whisper, weaving into it in a beautiful way, psalms and hymns and verses. She did not speak much of her religion beyond praising the goodness in others and being tender towards their weakness.

A. M. Allchin, *A Taste of Liberty*, p. 2

The prayer of general thanksgiving is still a useful framework, sketching out what it is for which we should praise God:

- our creation, preservation, and all the blessings of this life;

- God's immeasurable love in giving Jesus to die for us;

- the means of grace and the hope of glory.

Everything for which we should be thankful can be fitted into the structure of the prayer.

> *Almighty God, Father of all mercies,*
> *we your unworthy servants give you most*
> *humble and hearty thanks*
> *for all your loving kindness*
> *to us and to all people.*
> *We bless you for our creation, preservation,*
> *and all the blessings of this life;*
> *but above all for your immeasurable love*
> *in the redemption of the world by our*
> *Lord Jesus Christ,*
> *for the means of grace, and for the hope of glory.*
> *And give us, we pray, such a sense of all*
> *your mercies*
> *that our hearts may be unfeignedly thankful,*
> *and that we show forth your praise,*
> *not only with our lips but in our lives,*
> *by giving up ourselves to your service,*
> *and by walking before you in holiness*
> *and righteousness all our days;*
> *through Jesus Christ our Lord,*
> *to whom with you and the Holy Spirit,*
> *be all honour and glory,*
> *for ever and ever. Amen*

Praise promotes growth in the Spirit and puts us in touch with the divine creativity which God willingly shares with us. In turn this promotes and stimulates and enables every aspect of human creativity. Praise of God overflows into science and music, and art, literature, and poetry. At their best, all human creative achievements are a testimony to the skills given to us by God and the attention we give back to him.

But when we manage to focus on God, perhaps for only a moment, and begin to respond with praise, do not be surprised if immediately we are left tongue-tied. This is one of the ways of checking that we are not caught in the cul-de-sac of self but are truly approaching God. "What can I say, my God, my Holy Joy?" asks St Augustine, "what can any man say when he speaks of Thee?" Silence and a deep awareness of human frailty are the authentic beginnings of praise and adoration even though they look blank and unpromising. The glory is that out of this space God himself gives us words of praise to say and new songs to sing.

DOROTHY L. SAYERS

The American evangelist Billy Graham asked the question, "If you were arrested for being a Christian, would there be enough evidence to convict you?" Dorothy L. Sayers (1893–1958) was well known as a writer of detective stories and the creator of the sleuth Lord Peter Wimsey. Yet her best work provides plenty of evidence to convince us of her faith. She has been one of the most valuable witnesses for Christ in the twentieth century. Her plays, especially the series written for the BBC, *The Man Born to be King*, were said to "have done more for the preaching of the Gospel to the unconverted than any other single effort of the Churches".

She also wrote a number of popular books of theology and articles, vigorously expounding Christian ideas, and applying them to daily life and contemporary issues. She was a friend of Archbishop William Temple, and at his invitation took part in the famous Malvern Conference in 1941 which attempted to prepare the churches in England for the task which would face them once the Second World War was over. She wrote religious plays for Canterbury Cathedral and Lichfield Cathedral, and spent much of the last years of her life translating a great spiritual classic *The Divine Comedy* by Dante.

Dorothy L. Sayers was often outrageous and controversial in spite of her ecclesiastical and academic background – her father was a parish priest in the Fens and she had a brilliant career at Oxford. She had what she herself called a careless rage for life, and as we shall see she could never abide any dull presentations of Christianity or lifeless portraits of Jesus and his friends.

Perhaps it seems unusual to put her alongside Mary, but, like Mary, Dorothy Sayers' faith grew out of her knowledge of Jesus and a strongly held doctrine of the incarnation; things which she too pondered often in her heart. Her life had its dark side. She knew considerable personal suffering and pain, giving birth to an illegitimate child, and remaining loyal to her husband when his health collapsed and he became virtually totally dependent on her. Her faith was not arrived at easily or held comfortably, and she constantly brought it face to face with doubt and argument, dispute and debate, but it survived and grew and enabled her to go on praising God throughout her life. Her praise of God was firmly based on her knowledge of Jesus, and her thankful acknowledgement that he is the Saviour of the World, the Man born to be King.

Here is a fine passage describing Jesus, written with great energy and clarity for an article in *The Sunday Times* in 1938. Although it is rather long, it is worth reading carefully and in full. Out of such a lively faith can spring many prayers of praise.

> *The Christian faith is the most exciting drama that ever staggered the imagination of man – and the dogma is the drama. That drama is summarised quite clearly in the creeds of the Church, and if we think it dull it is because we either have never really read those amazing documents or have recited them so often and so mechanically as to have lost all sense of their meaning. The plot pivots upon a single character, and the whole action is the answer to a single central problem:* What think ye of Christ?

> *The Church's answer is categorical and uncompromising, and it is this: That Jesus Bar-Joseph, the carpenter of Nazareth, was in fact and in truth, and in the most exact and literal sense of the words, the God "by whom all things were made". His body and brain were those of a common man; his personality was the personality of God, so far as that personality could be expressed in human terms. He was not a demon pretending to be human; he was in every respect a genuine living man. He was not merely a man so good as to be "like God" – he was God. This is the dogma we find so dull – this terrifying drama of which God is the victim and hero.*

> *If this is dull, then what, in heaven's name, is worthy to be called exciting? The people who hanged Christ never, to do them justice, accused him of being a bore – on the contrary,*

they thought him too dynamic to be safe. It has been left for later generations to muffle up that shattering personality and surround him with an atmosphere of tedium. We have very efficiently pared the claws of the Lion of Judah, certified him "meek and mild", and recommended him as a fitting household pet for pale curates and pious old ladies. To those who knew him, however, he in no way suggested a milk-and-water person; they objected to him as a dangerous firebrand. True, he was tender to the unfortunate, patient with honest inquirers, and humble before Heaven; but he insulted respectable clergymen by calling them hypocrites. He referred to king Herod as "that fox"; he went to parties in disreputable company and was looked upon as a "gluttonous man and a winebibber", a friend of publicans and sinners; he assaulted indignant tradesmen and threw them and their belongings out of the temple; he drove a coach-and-horses through a number of sacrosanct and hoary regulations; he cured diseases by any means that came to hand, with a shocking casualness in the matter of other people's pigs and property; he showed no proper deference for wealth or social position; when confronted with neat dialectical traps, he displayed a paradoxical humour that affronted serious-minded people, and he retorted by asking disagreeable searching questions that could not be answered by rule of thumb. He was emphatically not a dull man in his human lifetime, and if he was God, there can be nothing dull about God either.

"And the third day he rose again". *What are we to make of this? One thing is certain if he were God and nothing else, his immortality means nothing to us; if he was man and no more, his death is no more important than yours or mine. But if he really was both God and man, then when the man Jesus died, God died too: and when the God Jesus rose from the dead, man rose too, because they were one and the same person ... there is the essential doctrine, of which the whole elaborate structure of Christian faith and morals is only the logical consequence. Now we may call that doctrine exhilarating, or we may call it devastating; we may call it a revelation, or we may call it rubbish; but if we call it dull, then words have no meaning at all.*

Dorothy Sayers shows clearly how Christian praise can grow from
our energetic enjoyment of life, especially when it is lived in
Christ, who says to all his friends, "I have come that you may have
life – life in all its fullness" (John 10.10).

MARY

Use St Luke's Gospel to read about Mary because it records most,
although not all, of the events in her life. Luke was writing for
gentiles living in the Greek world some years after the death of
Jesus, but in his first two chapters he recaptures and describes
beautifully the Jewish world as it was at the time of Jesus' birth,
roughly slightly more than half a century earlier.

Luke could not have known that world for himself at first hand,
and some Christians have suggested he came to know Mary in her
old age and gathered information about it from her. Whether or not
this is the case, Luke describes a time of intense hope, anticipation,
and longing. Many Jews, including Elizabeth and Zechariah, the
parents of John the Baptist, and Mary and Joseph were waiting for
what they called "the redemption of Israel" – the time when God
would send his messiah and bring in his kingdom.

The first mention of Mary (Luke 1.27) is when she became
aware that God wanted her to be the mother of Jesus. For a Jew, it
was inevitable that a message from God required a messenger
(in Greek *angelos*), and so Gabriel comes to Mary. Incredibly,
Mary is faced with the announcement that her child will be part of
God's messianic purpose. She would have been taught about God's
purposes and her nation's history, but she would never have
dreamed that she would be the one chosen to bring to an end a
huge historical process and set another in motion. The birth of her
son would wind up pages of the past and bring a new era.

Having come to terms with such a momentous thought, and
having pondered the many questions it brought, Mary is given "a
new song to sing" – Magnificat – words which have become one of
the most popular of all Christian songs of praise:

> *Tell out, my soul, the greatness of the Lord:*
> *unnumbered blessings, give my spirit voice;*
> *Tender to me the promise of his word;*
> *in God my Saviour shall my heart rejoice.*

Most of the words came to her from the Scriptures she knew well (what we call the Old Testament). Compare Luke 1.46–55, the Song of Mary, with 1 Samuel 2.1–10, the Song of Hannah. Then look at another song in the Bible which is less well known, but has similar themes. During his exile in Babylon, against the direct command of King Nebuchadnezzar, Daniel sang praise to God using words which he, too, says came to him in a vision:

> *Blessed be the name of God for ever and ever,*
> *to whom belong wisdom and might.*
> *He changes times and seasons;*
> *he removes kings and sets up kings;*
> *he gives wisdom to the wise*
> *and knowledge to those who have understanding;*
> *he reveals deep and mysterious things;*
> *he knows what is in the darkness,*
> *and the light dwells with him.*
> *To thee, O God of my fathers,*
> *I give thanks and praise,*
> *For thou hast given me wisdom and strength,*
> *and hast now made known to me what we asked of*
> *thee.*

Daniel 2.20–23

Now trace the themes which are common to each of these songs of praise:

- God's eternity and greatness;

- his sovereignty over all creation, including kings and nations, the mighty and humble alike;

- his providence which sustains and orders the world, and brings to fulfilment his purpose within it;

- his relationship with individual men and women whom he knows, and calls and loves and equips to serve him.

Whenever Christians praise God, either in music or speech, in activity or silence, they continue to weave together Bible texts and teaching and apply them to our own times. Many well-known Christian songs are examples: "All people that on earth do dwell" is a paraphrase of Psalm 100; "Praise my soul, the King of heaven" is a paraphrase of Psalm 103; "O worship the King" is a paraphrase of Psalm 104. You might like to write a song or prayer of praise using some or all of these themes, and use it in worship.

In one of her plays, Dorothy L. Sayers gives these words to Mary:

> *When the Angel's message came to me, the Lord put a song into my heart. I suddenly saw that wealth and cleverness were nothing to God – no one is too unimportant to be his friend. That was the thought that came to me, because of the thing that happened to ME. I am quite humbly born, yet the Power of God came upon me; very foolish and unlearned, yet the Word of God was spoken to me; and I was in deep distress, when my baby was born and filled my life with love. So I know very well that Wisdom and Power and Sorrow can live together with Love; and for me, the child in my arms is the answer to all the riddles.*

> *The Man Born to be King*

Part of Mary's praise of God and offering of adoration enabled her to provide a secure and loving home for Jesus. But as her child grew, Mary had other lessons to learn, other opportunities for personal growth in praying. Motherhood would not always be a simple matter of praise. Mary had to turn some painful experiences into the raw material of praise. In an ancient tradition, Mary's five joyful mysteries are followed by her five sorrowful mysteries, reminding us of how much her prayers of praise embraced.

There were various Jewish customs associated with childbirth, and one of them required Mary and Joseph to take their new baby to the temple at Jerusalem. While they carried Jesus into the temple, Simeon prophesied about him.

> *Behold this child is set for the fall and rising of many in Israel, and for a sign that is spoken against (and a sword will pierce through your own soul also), that thoughts out of many hearts may be revealed.*

> Luke 2.34–35

Again, not many years after, Mary suffered distress when Jesus was lost in the temple and she looked for him anxiously. When the boy was found, she was angry.

> *"Son, why have you treated us so? Behold your father and I have been looking for you anxiously." And he said to them,*

"How is it that you sought me? Did you not know that I must be in my Father's house?" And they did not understand the saying which he had spoken to them.

Luke 2.48–50

While Jesus was growing through boyhood and adolescence, Luke says Mary "kept all these things and pondered them in her heart" (Luke 2.19, 51). Christian praise cannot escape the pain of reality or refuse to face the facts. Instead, it looks at the places of pain and suffering, and at the harsh facts which tell against faith, trying to find something there which is of God and which can be taken out of the distress and anguish and used when we approach him in praise and adoration.

Mary believed God's word in spite of her uncertainty and her searching question, "How can this be?". Her trust in God and her willing obedience became not only the seeds of her songs of praise but also the source of her humility and confidence. These two things sound like opposites. How can humility become confidence? We see it happening in Mary.

Usually we think humility is self-denigration, which it isn't. Mary's humility is self-emptying and obedience and through it she is filled with great confidence in the Spirit. Christians are often enfeebled because they are not living through that particular growth point. The two qualities do not conflict. Combined as they should be, and as they were in Mary, they produce a remarkable aspect of the Christian character, a quiet serenity which copes with suffering and disappointment as much as with joy and strength. Another follower of Jesus, St Paul, discovered the same and wrote, "I can do all things – in Christ who strengthens me" (Philippians 4.13).

READINGS

1. O praise ye the Lord

Can any praise be worthy of the Lord's majesty? How magnificent his strength! How inscrutable his wisdom! Man is one of your creatures, Lord, and his instinct is to praise you. He bears about him the mark of death, the sign of his own sin, to remind him that you Thwart the proud. But still, since he is a part of your creation, he wishes to praise you. The thought of you stirs him so deeply that he cannot be content unless he praises you, because you made him for yourself and our hearts find no peace until they rest in you.

Grant me, Lord, to know and understand whether a man is first to pray to you for help or to praise you, and whether he must know you before he can call you to his aid.

Those who look for the Lord will cry out in praise of him, because all who look for him shall find him, and when they find him they will praise him. I shall look for you, Lord, by praying to you and as I pray I shall believe in you.

St Augustine, *Confessions* 1.1

2.   The joy of God's love

It is an inestimable joy that I was raised out of nothing to see and enjoy this glorious world; it is a sacred gift whereby the children of men are made my treasures, but O thou who art fairer than the children of men, how great and inconceivable is the joy of thy love.

That I who was so lately raised out of dust, have so great a friend, that I who in this life am born to mean things according to the world, should be called to inherit such great things in the way of heaven, such a Lord, so great a lover, such heavenly mysteries, such doings and such sufferings, with all the benefit and pleasure of them in thy intelligible Kingdom; it amazeth, it transporteth, it ravisheth me.

I will leave my father's house and come unto thee, for thou art my Lord and I will worship thee.

Traherne, *Centuries* 1.92

3.   Freedom from self-centredness

Perhaps the greatest of the things which the discipline of corporate worship does for those who submit to its influence is that it delivers them from that cramping tendency to self-occupation by which nearly all human beings – and especially pious human beings – are beset: MY soul, MY spiritual life, MY sins, MY problems, MY communion with God. All true and important facts no doubt; but facts that get on best, like many hardy annuals, if well thinned out in the first instance and then left to themselves. All that sort of thing is drowned in a great common act of praise and joy; a common act of communion and self-dedication.

Evelyn Underhill, *The Mount of Purification*

4. Jesus and his mother

And then he brought our Blessed Lady to mind. In my spirit I saw her as though she were physically present, a simple humble girl, still in her youth, and little more than a child. God showed me something of her spiritual wisdom and honesty, and I understood her profound reverence when she saw her God and maker; how reverently she marvelled that he should be born of his own creature, and of one so simple. This wisdom and honesty, which recognised the greatness of her Creator and the smallness of her created self, moved her to say to Gabriel in her utter humility, "Behold the handmaid of the Lord!" By this I knew for certain that in worth and grace she is above all that God made, save the blessed humanity of Christ.

Julian of Norwich, *Revelations of Divine Love*, 4.1

(Note: During Mother Julian's lifetime and generally in the Middle Ages, Mary was often described as *Our Blessed Lady* and the phrase is still used by many Christians today.)

5. A song of creation

The other said, "Caedmon, you must sing to me."
Caedmon broke into a cry of pain
To know it was that, and he must fail again,
And yet to know nonetheless that it had to be.

He asked, "What can I sing? I could not learn the lays."
  The grave answer came, "Sing of what you know.
  Tell how God commanded and it was so.
Sing of creation; praise as you have longed to praise!"

"Will you teach me?" Caedmon asked, half fearing,
  And for comfort, or faith, put out his hand
  To touch the other where he felt him stand;
And at that touch the night burst, shuddering.

Then the primeval dark overtook Caedmon.
  The darkness always lying beyond the firelight,
  Unthawed midwinter, everlasting midnight;
He was afraid to find himself so alone,

Falling into the night before existence.
  The depths of silence opened endlessly;
  There was nothing but perpetual journey;
Till he thought a voice sang out, far in the distance.

And the joy broke, the vision came with power.
  The frozen sky unfolded into arches
  Where the trees of heaven sent their shimmering branches;
He saw the angel of creation rise in fire;

And within him too the songmaker's passion mounted.
  His voice was borne on the cry that both upheld it
  And even into its own mighty utterance bound it;
He could not help but sing; it was commanded.

Caroline Glyn, Caedmon

6. The Song of the Three Children

*The symbol of the Church's praise of God is always the
Song of the Three Children as they plunged into the fiery
furnace, bidding all creatures praise the Lord and magnify
him for ever (the song is found in full in The Apocrypha). It
lays upon us an obligation to praise God through the
furnace. Not easy, for mind and heart, if they are alive,
must be aware of things which cry to high heaven in the
world and seem to defy the very name of God. And in your
heart perhaps there is sorrow and anxiety. Even in these*

*there are things that rouse us to praise – for instance the
touching heroism and endurance of our fellow beings.*

E. K. Talbot, *Retreat Addresses*

7. If ......

*If my lips could sing as many songs
as there are waves in the sea:
if my tongue could as many hymns
as there are ocean billows:
if my mouth
filled the whole firmament with praise
if my face
shone like the sun and moon together:
if my hands
were to hover in the like sky powerful eagles
and my feet
ran across mountains as swiftly as the deer;
all that would not be enough
to pay you fitting tribute,
O Lord my God.*

Hymn probably composed in the Talmudic period,
3rd–5th century AD

8. The spirit of praise

*God loves us with a love beyond words, and leaves us
free to make a radical choice: free to love or to refuse
to love and to reject God; free to spread through the world
a leaven of reconciliation or a ferment of injustice; free
to shine with radiant communion in Christ or to tear
ourselves away from it and even to destroy in others their
thirst for the living God.*

*But God does not look on passively at the choices of
human beings. God suffers along with them. Through
Christ, in agony for each man and woman on this earth,
by his Holy Spirit constantly active within us, God visits
us even in the deserts of our hearts.*

*Together with Mary, turned towards the Risen Christ, we
can wait in the peace of our nights, in the silence of our
days, in the beauty of creation and in times of deep inner
struggle – wait for our deserts to flower.*

Brother Roger of Taizé

PRAYERS

1. Adoration

*In these three words, "joy, happiness, and eternal
delight", I was shown three heavens. By "joy" I
understand the pleasure experienced by the Father;
"happiness", the work of the Son; "eternal delight", the
Holy Spirit. The Father is pleased, the Son is
worshipped, the Holy Spirit is delighted. It is the will of
God that we too should delight with him in our salvation,
and thereby be greatly comforted and strengthened.*

Julian of Norwich, *Revelations of Divine Love*;
chapter 23

Opening yourself more deeply and fully to the
presence of God, ask him to fill your heart and mind
with praise.

2. Penitence

*We know from our creeds, and believe through the
teaching and preaching of Holy Church, that the
blessed Trinity makes mankind in his image and
likeness. In the same way we know that when man
fell so deeply and wretchedly through sin there was
no other help forthcoming to restore him but from
him who made man.*

Julian of Norwich, *Revelations of Divine Love*;
chapter 10

Think of the cross and the Gospel: "Christ died for
our sins" that we might be "ransomed, healed,
restored, forgiven", and ask God to make you
penitent and able to receive his love and forgiveness.

3.   Intercession

In this way I saw how Christ has compassion on us because of our sin. And just as previously I had been full of sorrow and compassion at the sight of his suffering, so now I was filled with compassion for all my fellow Christians, those people greatly beloved and saved, the servants of God. For Holy Church shall be shaken at the world's sorrow, anguish, and tribulation, just as men shake a cloth in the wind.

Julian of Norwich, *Revelations of Divine Love*;
chapter 28

Pray for all those you know who suffer in any way and pray for all those who help them, asking God to show you the way in which you too can help in the name of Jesus.

4.   Dedication

God showed me too the pleasure it gives him when a simple soul comes to him, openly, sincerely, and genuinely. It seems to me as I ponder this revelation that when the Holy Spirit touches the soul it longs for God rather like this: "God, of your goodness give me yourself, for you are sufficient for me. I cannot properly ask anything less, to be worthy of you. If I were to ask less, I should always be in want. In you alone do I have all".

Julian of Norwich, *Revelations of Divine Love*;
chapter 5

Allow God to give you true contentment and refreshment as he is with you, loving you, holding you, and receiving you to himself.

5.   *Written Prayers*

O God, whose love we cannot measure, nor even number your blessings: we bless and praise you for all your goodness, who in our weakness is our strength, in our darkness, light, in our sorrows, comfort and peace, and from everlasting so everlasting remains our God, Father, Son and Holy Spirit, world without end. Amen

O praise the Lord with me,
*   and let us magnify his name together.*
I will sing unto the Lord as long as I live,
*   I will praise my God while I have my being.*
O give thanks unto the Lord, for he is gracious;
*   and his mercy endureth for ever.*

Psalm 34.104, 107

Blessed be thou, Lord God,
*   our Father, for ever and ever.*
Thine, O Lord, is the greatness
*   and the might and the glory*
and the victory and the majesty;
for all that is in heaven
*   and in the earth is thine;*
thine is the kingdom,
and thou art exalted as head over all.

King David (1 Chronicles 29)

3 THE FEARFUL VOID
EMPTINESS

INTRODUCTION

The desert in the garden and the garden in the desert (T. S. Eliot, "Ash Wednesday 1930")

Usually our picture of a desert is the Sahara with its great tracts of sand. There are though many quite different areas of the world, where there is no sand, which are still rightly and officially designated desert. The essential definition of a desert is a place which is uncultivated and barren.

> *The desert is not remote in southern tropics,*
> *The desert is not only around the corner,*
> *The desert is squeezed in the tube-train next to you,*
> *The desert is in the heart of your brother.*

> T. S. Eliot, Choruses from *"The Rock"*

Eliot uses the image of the desert with its meaning of uncultivated and barren to come to terms with the spiritual desolation which is too often all around us, and which the soulless city inflicts on us. "My factory is my desert" has become a slogan in our age. But it could be many other places: my high-rise block of flats, or my hospital ward, or my home now that my partner has deserted me. Desolation and emptiness are not inviting prospects and we fear them, but they have never been dismissed as totally destructive and negative in the search for spiritual growth.

Significantly, Elijah, John the Baptist, and Jesus all began their public ministry as prophets of God's Kingdom suddenly, coming as it were from nowhere, arriving from the wilderness and desert. Elijah came from Tishbe, away to the north-east of Israel, beyond the famous Cherith brook which is a tributary of the River Jordan. John the Baptist appeared further south in the Judean wilderness. Jesus too spent time in the wilderness, undergoing a battle with temptation, before he began preaching in Nazareth and Galilee. Like every Jew, these men looked back to the never-to-be-forgotten forty years in the wilderness, which was at the heart of their nation's history, and saw how God drew his people to himself and kept them close to him. Finding such positive hope in such dead surroundings makes the toughest demands on faith. But wilderness years or periods of emptiness are part of every disciple's journey and they can always be creative for his or her spirituality.

> *Blessed is the man whose strength is in thee: in*
> *whose heart are thy ways.*
> *Who going through the vale of misery use it for a*
> *well: and the pools are filled with water'.*

Psalm 84.5–6

Even among these rocks, our peace is his will (T. S. Eliot, "Ash Wednesday 1930")

There are perhaps at least three kinds of emptiness we can identify, which we have to live with and live through. There is the blank wall, reaching rock bottom, facing the total absence of God and all spiritual quickening. Then there are feelings of complete emptiness which sweep over us when we are very conscious of our nothingness, our powerlessness and our wretchedness. And then there is an emptiness which is deliberately sought because of a deep desire to meet with God. Before he became a preacher and missionary St Paul went into the desert of Arabia to reflect on what had happened to him and to prepare for what lay ahead (Galatians 1.17).

We experience each of these types of wilderness in our praying because they are part of what it means to be with God, and because God himself has to be "in the wilderness" if he is to be God. Eliot in his poem warns us, "you neglect and belittle the desert". Every Christian is called to go into all the places of wilderness and bring new life to them and fulfil the ancient words of promise from the Old Testament.

> *The wilderness and the dry land shall be glad,*
> *the desert shall rejoice and blossom;*
> *like the crocus, it shall blossom abundantly,*
> *and rejoice with joy and singing.*

Isaiah 35.1–2

I will give you treasures from dark vaults,
hoarded in secret places,
that you may know that I am the Lord,
Israel's God who calls you by name.

Isaiah 45.3

John Harvard, an English clergyman, went to Massachusetts, USA, in the seventeenth century to be a preacher. Within a year he had died of consumption, but he left money and books to form the nucleus of what has become Harvard University. He said he wanted to create a college in the wilderness, which as we know is exactly what he did and it is now one of the great universities of the world. He had enabled a wilderness to blossom abundantly. As we shall see, Trevor Huddleston did the same by bringing justice and love into the desert of apartheid in South Africa.

God promises to answer prayer; he promises "I will be there" whenever we turn to him. He is now with us in Christ to the end of time, but this presence does not mean God is constantly available to us in the forms and expectations we create and conceive. Instead there are times when God withdraws, when he hides himself, when there is a cloud of unknowing which is impenetrable. Praying always goes through occasions when God's presence has to be known in his absence. It sounds too paradoxical to be taken seriously. It sounds like a clever play on words. But it isn't so different from all person to person contact. We train ourselves to know the presence of the other when he or she is not immediately or tangibly with us.

Teach us to care and not to care
Teach us to sit still
Even among these rocks,
Our peace is his will.

T. S. Eliot, "*Ash Wednesday*"

Tears may endure for a night but joy comes in the morning (Psalm 30.5)

Carlo Carretto, who went to live with the Little Brothers of Charles de Foucauld in the desert, writes in one of his letters:

It was the decisive call. And I never understood it so deeply as on that evening at the Vespers of St Charles in 1954, when I said "yes" to the voice.

"Come with me into the desert". There is something much greater than human action: prayer; and it has a power much stronger than the words of men: love.

And I went into the desert.

The early Christian desert fathers in the fourth century left the security of city life and society, and deliberately went out into the deserts of Egypt, Palestine, Arabia, and Persia. Contrary to what we usually imagine, they were not looking for an escape to peace and quiet. Instead they went out into their wildernesses because they believed the conflict between good and evil, between God and Satan, between the power of God's Kingdom and the destructive forces opposed to it, was concentrated more powerfully away from civilization, at the fringes of the world, than within it. To make a stand for God was sharper and more painful in such an environment, and so, when they were given, the blessings were greater. Elijah, John the Baptist, and Jesus found in their solitariness "the point of conflict where good and evil meet", but they also saw the dawn of a new age and the sovereignty of God in action.

In our own century much spirituality has been produced by facing the emptiness within and seeking God there. A surprising number of people have gone into solitude and accepted the hermit life in the twentieth century and they strengthen us to face such times with courage. On the whole nowadays there is little need to go looking for the harsh and empty places. Many people's everyday experience brings them immediately and unremittingly into touch with them. What is required is the faith and determination to look them in the face and turn them from minus into plus, to see them as part of the cross and resurrection of Jesus.

"You must strip your prayers," the novice-master told me. You must simplify, deintellectualise. Put yourself in front of Jesus as a poor man: not with any big ideas, but with living faith. Remain motionless in an act of love before the Father. Don't try to reach God with your understanding: that is impossible. Reach him in love; that is possible.

Carlo Carretto, *Letters from the Desert*, pp. 12 and 13

TREVOR HUDDLESTON

In a famous book *Naught for your Comfort* published in 1956 which sold rapidly throughout the world, Father Trevor Huddleston, a parish priest in South Africa as he then was, said:

> *Prophecy is a function of the Church, and must be so till the end of time, for it will always be the duty of the Church to proclaim that this world is God's world and that infringements of his law will bring their own terrible penalties.*

Naught for your Comfort, p. 239

Since writing those words, Trevor Huddleston has become a bishop and an archbishop, but it is his experience in South Africa which remains the key to his Christian ministry. He stands along-side Elijah in the same prophetic tradition. He has denounced injustice and evil openly and vigorously. He has stood against the State, and done all he could to claim it and bring it within God's rule and sovereignty. Also, as we shall see, he too fled for his life, and he has spent much of life feeling exiled from the place he loves most.

Trevor Huddleston was born in 1913. As a young man he was greatly influenced by the Christian Socialist movement whose members worked especially in the London slums, trying to mitigate the endemic poverty they found there and to awaken the consciences of the privileged and well-to-do. At Oxford, he read history and afterwards trained for ordination. Then he joined the Community of the Resurrection at Mirfield, an Anglican religious order in West Yorkshire. The monks live under monastic vows and Huddleston took his vows in 1941.

In 1943 he was sent to South Africa to take charge of the Community Mission, centred on the Church of Christ the King in the black township of Sophiatown, Johannesburg. In 1949 he was appointed Provincial of the Order, with headquarters a few miles away in white Rosettenville. In this position, he was also responsible for St Peter's School (sometimes called the black Eton) and for the Theological College. During this time he also did what he could to make some relaxation and recreation possible for the blacks in the townships – the Odin Cinema was opened in Sophiatown and the Huddleston Swimming Baths built in Orlando, and visiting musicians were persuaded to give concerts.

Archbishop Desmond Tutu remembers these days:

*He was so un-English in many ways, being very fond of
hugging people, embracing them, and in the way he
laughed. He did not laugh like many white people, only
with their teeth, he laughed with his whole body, his
whole being, and that endeared him very much to black
people. And if he wore a white cassock it did not remain
clean for long, as he trudged the dusty streets of
Sophiatown.*

However, the accession to power in 1948 of the National Party,
with its avowed intent not only to strengthen the existing colour
bar, but to entrench it by legislation, made confrontation and
protest inevitable. Some of the government legislation was such
that to accept it without protest would have meant dishonour to the
principles at the heart of Huddleston's religious life and betrayal
of the blacks he served. Two areas of protest were especially
provoking to the government – first his well-publicized protest at
the removal of blacks (who had freehold rights) from Sophiatown
and, second, his decision to close down the school rather than hand
it over to government control and a syllabus designed to train
blacks for inferiority. The government and its supporters were glad
to see him leave in 1956.

Strictly speaking he was not evicted or sent into exile, nor was
his life threatened, but he was deliberately recalled home to his
community at Mirfield in Yorkshire and he felt it very deeply. The
first thing he did was to put down his feelings on paper.

*This book, written from the heart of the Africa I love, would
be incomplete if I did not somehow see it in the context of
this sudden, unwanted, but inevitable departure: "Partir,
c'est mourir un peu"… and I am in the process of dying: in
the process "every hour". The thing about such a death;
the quality of it is to heighten the loveliness of what one is
leaving behind. Without sentimentality or any foolish
regrets, it is most necessary to try and evaluate one's
feelings: to try to discover and relate that strange but
deeply real truth which so many have experienced – the
witchery of Africa: the way it lays hold on your heart and
will not let you go.*

Naught for your Comfort, pp. 13–14

This was the book which brought to the attention of the world the
evil of racial conflict and it is at least one of the principal factors in

South Africa's history which has brought to birth hope for a just and equal society and an end to racial discrimination.

Compare this next paragraph written by Trevor Huddleston in *Naught for your Comfort* with the words of Elijah which follow:

> *The Church of South Africa seems to me to stand at the parting of the ways. It will not be the first time in her history that she is confronted with a choice: indeed it is a choice which from the beginning has been present, fronting both the individual and the Divine Society of which he is a member.*

> *Elijah came near to all the people and said, "How long will you go limping with two different opinions? If the Lord is God, follow him; but if Baal, then follow him." And the people did not answer a word.*

1 Kings 18.21

Elijah drew his strength from his "waiting on God" and his trust in God's presence. Someone who knew Trevor Huddleston in South Africa says of him:

> *I know he is a man of very deep prayer and that is what sustained him in his campaigns to alleviate the sorry lot of the people that he loved so dearly.*

> *I have no religious faith, but when I look at that photograph [of Huddleston] of a profoundly religious man, I see godliness in a way I can understand deeply, I see a man in whom prayer functions, in Simone Weil's definition, as a special form of intelligent concentration.*

Simone Weil had defined prayer and action like this.

> *Prayer consists of attention. Not only does the love of God have attention for its substance; the love of our neighbour, which we know to be the same love, is made of the same substance. The capacity to give one's attention to a sufferer is a very rare and difficult thing; it is almost a miracle; it is a miracle ... Warmth of heart ... pity, are not enough.*

Simone Weil, *Waiting on God*, pp. 51, 58

ELIJAH

St Mark records how when Peter, James, and John saw the vision of the transfiguration of Jesus, they also saw Moses and Elijah talking with him. For Jews they were the traditional representatives of the two pillars of their religion – their Law and their Prophets (Mark 9.2–8). But who was Elijah, and why was he still remembered in the time of Jesus?

Begin by recalling briefly the main events in Elijah's life. They can be found in 1 Kings 17—2 Kings 2.

- He arrives at the court of King Ahab (King of Israel 869–850 BC) and Queen Jezebel, and warns the people of a severe drought which will only end at a time of God's choosing.

- He goes away beyond the River Jordan and is fed by the ravens, a sign of God's providence and care.

- He stays with the widow at Zarephath and God sustains them both; and later Elijah restores her child to her.

- He goes to Mount Carmel and challenges the prophets of Baal; after the contest the people affirm, "the Lord, he is God".

- He escapes Queen Jezebel's anger and flees for his life to Mount Horeb where he hears God's voice speaking to him.

- He pronounces judgement against King Ahab for injustice in having Naboth killed in battle in order to obtain possession of his vineyard.

- Finally, tradition says, Elijah "was taken up to heaven in a whirlwind".

When the three disciples were returning home with Jesus from the mountain of the transfiguration, they asked him about Elijah, "Why do the scribes say that first Elijah must come?" The disciples had in mind a passage in the last chapter of the Old Testament, "Behold, I will send you Elijah the prophet before the great and terrible day of the Lord comes" (Malachi 4.5).

Jesus' reply shows that he understood Elijah to have been a man with a mission from God and a prophet of God's Kingdom. "Elijah does come first" he said, "to restore all things". The restoration of all things – putting things right, restoring them to their proper place within the divine order of creation – is among the events which

Jesus believed would lead to the coming of God's Kingdom, and much of his ministry was shaped by this belief. Look again at the list of the main events in Elijah's life and see how each of them is in some way or another a declaration of God's judgement and salvation: a restoration of things broken and disordered. Clearly Elijah did not shirk his responsibility as a prophet of God's Kingdom and nor, of course, did Jesus. Think now of Jesus' public ministry and notice the parallels between his work and Elijah's. These shouldn't come as a surprise, bearing in mind that both were called by God and equipped by him to do his work of establishing his divine sovereignty over his creation.

Elijah defended and fought for God's justice and holiness. He pronounced judgement against King Ahab and Queen Jezebel, against the cult of Baal, and against the apostasy of his nation. The great drought was not brought to an end until he had confronted the prophets of Baal, and the people had returned to the worship of God, at least for a time, and had rejected the heathen cult (1 Kings 18.45). Afterwards Elijah fled for his life, because of the anger of Queen Jezebel. He went on a journey into the wilderness as far as Mount Horeb. He travelled "for forty days and forty nights", another significant echo of the forty years the Jews spent in the wilderness after their exodus from Egypt.

In the emptiness he confronted his fears and disappointments, believing that, in spite of his work, he had failed (1 Kings 19.4). Eventually God spoke to him and commissioned him further.

> *When Elijah heard [the still small voice] he wrapped his face in his mantle and went out and stood at the entrance of the cave. And behold there came a voice to him, and said, "What are you doing here, Elijah?" He said, I have been very jealous for the Lord, the God of hosts; for the people of Israel have forgotten thy covenant, thrown down thy altars, and slain thy prophets with the sword; and I, even I only, am left; and they seek my life, to take it away. And the Lord said to him, "Go, return on your way to the wilderness of Damascus and when you arrive, you shall anoint Hazael to be king over Syria; and Jehu the son of Nimshi you shall anoint to be king over Israel; and Elisha the son of Shaphat you shall anoint to be prophet in your place".*

1 Kings 19.13–16

Probably Jesus thought John the Baptist was a kind of "Elijah for his times". Certainly he recognized John's preaching as a prelude to his own ministry of preaching and healing, of proclaiming judgement and bringing forgiveness. He knew John had been put to death for denouncing Herod's sin, and in his conversation with the disciples he repeats, "I tell you that Elijah has come, and they did to him whatever they pleased, as it is written of him". Knowing too how Elijah had been exiled and threatened, and how John the Baptist had been put to death, Jesus must have known at least part of what happens to every faithful prophet of God's Kingdom.

From Elijah we learn:

• the need to stand against the state and society when necessary in the cause of truth and justice in the name of the Kingdom of God;

• the need to wait upon God, even at the cost of emptiness, disillusionment and the absence of hope, in order to hear God speaking.

READINGS

1. The still small voice

In 1930 a memorial window to Thomas Hardy was placed in the south aisle of Stinsford Church in Dorset where his heart lies buried. The subject of the window is Elijah on Horeb – one of Hardy's favourite Bible passages. The window is designed by Mr Douglas Strachen and vividly portrays the four elements of earth, water, air and fire with a dove as symbol of the Holy Spirit brooding over all.

Hardy's markings of favourite passages in his Bible ... have the air of being chosen not for poetical or religious reasons but because they have some personal application. Two passages are marked again and again, one in the Old Testament and one in the New. This first is among the verses in the First Book of Kings, chapter 19, which describes how Elijah came to hear the voice of God in the wilderness:

*"And he said, Go forth and stand upon the mount before
the Lord. And behold the Lord passed by, and a great
and strong wind rent the mountain, and brake in pieces
the rocks before the Lord; but the Lord was not in the
wind; and after the wind an earthquake; but the Lord
was not in the earthquake: And after the earthquake a
fire; but the Lord was not in the fire: and after the fire a
still small voice."*

*Hardy's second favourite passage was the fifteenth chapter
of the First Epistle to the Corinthians, which was... the
chapter on the resurrection, read at the service for the
burial of the dead.*

Robert Gittings, Young Thomas Hardy, p. 80

2.   A contemporary wilderness

*Consider the solitude of walking from the subway train
or bus to your house in the evening, when the streets
are quieter and there are few passersby. Consider the
solitude that greets you when you enter your room to
change your office or working clothes to more comfortable,
homey ones. Consider the solitude of the housewife, alone
in her kitchen, sitting down for a cup of coffee before
beginning the work of the day. Think of the solitude
afforded by such humble tasks as housecleaning, ironing,
sewing.*

*One of the first steps towards solitude is a departure. Were
you to depart to a real desert, you might take a plane or
a train or car to get there. But we're blind to the
"little departures" which fill our days. These "little
solitudes" are often right behind a door which we can
open, or in a little corner where we can stop to look at a
tree that somehow survived the snow and dust of a city
street. There is the solitude of a car in which we return
from work, riding bumper to bumper on a crowded
highway. This too can be a point of departure to a desert,
silence, solitude.*

Catherine de Hueck Doherty, Poustinia, p. 22

3. The true wilderness

*The wilderness belongs to us. It is always lurking
somewhere as part of our experience, and these are times
when it seems pretty near the whole of it. I'm not thinking
now of people being ostracised, or without friends, or
misunderstood. Objectively, as a matter of actual fact, these
things happen to very few of us. Most people's wilderness is
inside them, not outside. Thinking of it as outside is
generally a trick we play on ourselves – a trick to hide from
us what we really are, not comfortingly wicked, but
incapable, for the time being, of establishing communion.
Our wilderness, then, is an inner isolation. Its an absence
of contact. Its a sense of being alone – boringly alone, or
saddeningly alone, or terrifyingly alone.*

H. A. Williams, *The True Wilderness*, p. 29

4. Only man can fall

*Only man can fall from God
Only man.*

*No animal, no beast nor creeping thing
no cobra nor hyena nor scorpion nor hideous white ant
can slip entirely through the fingers of the hands of God
into the abyss of self-knowledge,
knowledge of the self-apart-from-God.*

*For the knowledge of the self-apart-from-God
is an abyss down which the soul can slip
writhing and twisting in all revolutions
of the unfinished plunge
of self-awareness, now apart from God, falling
fathomless, fathomless, self-conscious wriggling
writhing deeper and deeper in all the minutiae of
self-knowledge,
downward, exhaustive,
yet never, never going to the bottom, for there is no bottom;
zigzagging down like the fizzle from a finished rocket
the fizzling falling fire that cannot go out, dropping wearily,
neither can it reach the depth
for the depth is bottomless,*

as it wriggles its way even further down, further down
at last in sheer horror of not being able to leave off
knowing itself, knowing itself apart from God, falling.

D. H. Lawrence

5. A chapel in the Sahara

I climbed the last few feet of track to de Foucauld's chapel
on the top. It was a small square shed, dry-stone-walled
inside and out. The threshold was three steps up, from both
the ground outside and the chapel floor, to keep wind and
dust at bay.

An altar of rough stone, nothing but a supported slab, stood
free from the eastern wall. If you struck it sharply, it rang like
the stone on the hillside. Hanging from that wall was a Christ
figure, agonised in metal upon a crude stone cross, above a
segment of Tuareg leather work. Two thick candles stood in
brackets on either side and, to the right, the red lamp of the
Blessed Sacrament reserved. There was a Bible on a bracket
by the door, and an office book on another bracket attached to
the north wall. There was nothing else but an ikon above the
Bible. The floor was covered in rush matting, with four
goatskins on top. The roof of the chapel consisted of branches
held down by corrugated iron and stone. There were two
small windows, the only sources of light, one in the roof above
the altar, the other in the outer wall nearby.

I lay there for an hour or more undisturbed, before I moved
at all. I rose feeling tired, with a tide of depression lapping
gently round the ankles of my soul. Perhaps several days
here would have changed things, though I doubted it. I
went outside and stood for a little while on the tabletop of
Assekrem. The view was stupendous, with mountains rising
up like stalagmites all round. The wind came across the
summit in sweeping gusts, noisy and inflamed. There was a
sudden uprush beyond the end of the chapel: like smoke, a
flurry of dust rose into the air past the mountain's edge.
This was a holy place, and would have been even if no man
had ever trodden it.

Geoffrey Moorhouse, *The Fearful Void*, p. 284

6.   Wisdom from the desert

*A certain brother went to abbot Moses in Scete, and asked
him for a good word. And the elder said to him: Go, sit in
your cell, and your cell will teach you everything.*

Thomas Merton, *The Wisdom of the Desert*, p. 30

7.   An abyss

*My daughter had a very terrible illness, and it lasted for several
years, which was running concurrently with my husband dying.
I was in a very deep abyss really, and I felt I was at the
bottom. There I discovered that if you fight it, the abyss, if
you thrash around, and are struggling all the time, and feeling
this isn't where I should be, all you do is bruise yourself.*

*I discovered that the abyss is also worth exploring – or the
darkness, call it what you like. When you're in that state, if
you stop and look around, you become astonished at what you
do find. I found help in incredibly unexpected places – people
that I'd thought might be a help at that sort of time, when I felt
abandoned or in the abyss, actually were no help at all.
Instead, people I had not expected to help me, like my
daughter's teenage friends, for example, did help.*

Rosemary Hartill, *Were you There?*, p. 12

8.   If the Word is lost

*Where shall the word be found, where will the word
Resound? Not here, there is not enough silence
Not on the sea or on the islands, not
On the mainland, in the desert or the rain land,
For those who walk in darkness
Both in the day time and in the night time
The right time and the right place are not here
No place of grace for those who avoid the face
No time to rejoice for those who walk among noise and deny the
   voice.*

T. S. Eliot, "Ash Wednesday" 1930

PRAYERS

1. Adoration

> *Follow, poet, follow right*
> *To the bottom of the night,*
> *With your unconstraining voice*
> *Still persuade us to rejoice*

> W. H. Auden, In memory of W. B. Yeats

Begin with a resolve to follow Jesus wherever he leads, and ask him for his strength to find causes for thanksgiving everywhere, even in emptiness.

2. Penitence

> *An accidental happiness,*
> *Catching man off his guard, will blow him*
> *Out of his life in time to show him*
> *The fields of being where he may,*
> *Unconscious of Becoming, play*
> *With the Eternal Innocence*
> *In unimpeded Utterance.*
> *But perfect Being has ordained*
> *It must be lost to be regained,*
> *And in its orchards grow the tree*
> *And fruit of human destiny,*
> *And man must eat it and depart.*

> W. H. Auden, "New Year Letter 1940"

Admit your fear of emptiness and loneliness; then tell God of your failure and sin and ask him to be with you while you wait to be forgiven.

3.   Intercession

About suffering they were never wrong,
The Old Masters; how well they understood
Its human position; how it takes place
While someone else is eating or opening a window or just
*   walking dully along;*

W. H. Auden, "Musee des Beaux Arts"

Many people's suffering is made worse because they feel abandoned and forgotten; ask God to keep you mindful of all those in great distress and need and then pray for them.

4. Dedication

And because of His visitation, we may no longer desire
God as if He were lacking: our redemption is no longer
a question of pursuit but of surrender to him who is
always and everywhere present. Therefore at every
moment we pray that, following Him, we may depart
from our anxiety into His peace.

W. H. Auden, words of Simeon from "For the time being"

Whenever you are anxious and afraid, give yourself to God knowing that, even if he cannot remove its pain, he can does transform it and contain it within his blessing.

5.   Written Prayers

O Lord Jesus Christ
give us grace to grow in holiness,
to deny ourselves,
take up your cross
and follow you;
for your name's sake. Amen

Show me how to approach my sense of being alone and cut off so that it may not be any longer a condition to be dreaded, but rather seen as a means to closer dependence upon you. Let my soul learn in solitude the lesson of your presence.

"When lonely", from *A Book of Private Prayer*

Dear Lord, quieten my spirit and fix my thoughts on thy will, that I may see what thou wouldst have done, and contemplate its doing without self-consciousness or inner excitement, without haste and without delay, without fear of other people's judgements or anxiety about success, knowing only that it is thy will and therefore must be done quietly, faithfully and lovingly, for in thy will alone is our peace.

George Appleton

4 GOD OF ALL THE NATIONS
ACCEPTANCE

INTRODUCTION

Speak the truth in love (Ephesians 4.15)

Gerald Priestland, who used to be the BBC's religious affairs correspondent, once said when he looked back on his life, "I have not been half the things I wanted to be: a musician above all, a poet, a novelist, humorist, theologian. It took me 30 years to come to terms with the truth that I am a journalist". The moral is that before we attempt to speak the truth in love to others, we should make sure as far as we can we speak the truth to ourselves.

Truthfulness is at the heart of all discipleship and acceptance is an essential step in receiving it. With his usual common sense and deep spiritual perception, St Benedict knew that "unless and until he could live with himself he could not live with others, and conversely that unless he could live with others he could not live with himself" (Esther De Waal, *Living with Contradictions*, p. 51).

Acceptance has to be a foundation of all spiritual growth because our aim is to relate to the One who has created us. We did not choose to be born. We cannot choose the circumstances of our birth. We are not free to select the personality pluses and minuses which make us up. We sound hopelessly programmed and pre-packed which sets up all the wrong attitudes in us, especially when we are trying to relate to God. But these inevitable limitations need not be negative forces surrounding us. Once we accept this lack of freedom in a positive way, there is always the possibility of moving through and finding real freedom. There are plenty of choices we are free to make. We can choose between making good use and bad use of the raw material God gives us for living. We can choose either to accept or reject the opportunities within it which provide the space we require to develop. We can receive and welcome life in the Spirit which opens us to God's love or throw it away.

> *A life without acceptance is a life in which a most basic human need goes unfulfilled. Acceptance means that though there is need for growth I am not forced. I do not have to be the person I am not. Acceptance liberates everything that is in me. Only when I am loved in that deep sense of complete acceptance can I become myself.*

Our spirituality is deliberately set by God "in the flesh" and "in the world" because this is where he chooses to be himself. This radical immediacy:

> *brings us to the heart of prayer: letting yourself be open to everything that's there, but with God at the heart. We are not meant to be specialists in God, cutting out the world. This may be near the bone for clergy who focus on God alone – but what does "God alone" mean? The here and now, wide and broad is where we meet him. In the story of the young man, desperately listening for the bells of the sunken Cathedral, it was only when he gave up hope and expectation, no longer trying to hear the bells, that he truly heard the sound of the surf and the sea birds: and in their sound he heard the bells. So it is with God in prayer: we must be open to the whole range of voices which speak to us of God; and they may not be religious ones. God may speak through strange people, but if we don't listen and acknowledge, we are the poorer.*

Honest to God

Christians then should have no desire to escape reality and no regrets for it. This is where we are called to be and to serve, and from which we are invited to enter God's Kingdom in the here and now. We chase away the vague feelings of "if only" and the longing to be where, falsely, we imagine the grass is greener.

Nevertheless, this is no blanket resignation to "whatever will be will be". That kind of acceptance ceases to be productive and is destroyed by complacency or indifference. Once we recognize, though, that in accepting what God gives he opens up the ground of our being, then powerfully from it his Holy Spirit brings a crop – fruit which will last.

Looking into reality is not as simple as it sounds. To know ourselves takes time and a minor (or even a major) miracle of honesty, especially in an age where we are encouraged to achieve, to stand on our own two feet, to reckon ourselves of worth only if we are in competition and rivalry with everyone else around us. Christian spirituality approves of "running the race which is set before us" (Hebrews 12.1), but it has never stopped there. It has always balanced success and failure, and used them both for growth. "He has some promising weaknesses" is perhaps one of the most useful and accurate remarks written on a school report. Usually we have to work to establish the balance and our prayers should help us.

Someone said, "today there are too many good Christians when the world needs saints". Praying, like being a disciple, is often much simpler and more direct than we take it to be, but it is also much tougher and more demanding than we can ever imagine. It means taking penitence and resolution together, finding the way that evil is overcome by good, living through the tears to find joy. It means using all our moods as they change and whirl about us. It is worth collecting up the prayers of Christian men and women from every age through which they have expressed the full range of their feelings. Explore, too, the range of praying expressed in the Psalms (for instance compare the desolation of Psalm 102 with the praise of Psalm 103).

Effective praying is rooted in the capacity to be honest with oneself and honest with God. The famous prayer which reminds us that God knows us better than we do ourselves is the basis of this honesty. Using the discipline of sacramental confession is another powerful and creative way of facing the truth. There is no reason to pretend with God, because pretence is only another humanly devised screen from reality. We can say anything to God precisely because he knows it already. His fore-knowledge is sometimes taken to be an argument that prayer is unnecessary. In fact it provides real freedom which is the gateway to development, discovery, and renewal, until eventually because God is at work in us we can say quietly and confidently, "well I'm me, and it's all right".

The world needs nothing less than all the world

I have seen posters in many churches in France with those words on them, "*Le monde aura besoin de tout le monde*", inviting me to consider that unless and until I am in touch with all my fellow human beings, and accept them and their religious insights and integrity, I remain incomplete, and so do they.

The desire for deep unity, not only between Christians but also between people of all creeds and cultures and races, springs from this sense of incompleteness rather than from a desire to conquer or dominate others, or empire-build; or at least it should. Christianity has always been part of a larger whole – whether Christians have realized and accepted it or not. Jesus himself was a Jew, who grew up within a great religious heritage which he both affirmed and challenged.

Robert Runcie, while he was Archbishop of Canterbury, said at a conference in Calcutta to leaders of many faiths:

> *We must be humble and sincere enough to concede that there is some incompleteness and shortcoming in each of our traditions; that there is room and need for further growth in all of them.*

All those who seek God should be motivated by the same kind of humility and longing, which is an essential and creative part of love and produces the kind of loving that is strong enough to receive either rejection or response, patient enough to move at the speed of others, and enduring enough to go on and on.

The Christian Church has received many treasures of prayer and devotion from Judaism, as well as developing new ones of her own. The Jewish psalms are still central to virtually every act of Christian worship. Morning and evening prayer is founded on an ancient Jewish custom, and has developed from the worship of the synagogue. The great hymn "Holy, holy, holy" is from the temple and its worship. The Eucharist or Holy Communion has grown out of the fellowship meals of the Jews.

We know not all prayer is Christian prayer, and there are varieties of spirituality and devotion in the human approach and response to God. What is unique to the Christian way is that we approach God through Jesus Christ, a man about whom we may not know as much as we would like, but we do know enough to be sure he is firmly an historical person who taught his followers to call God "Father" and to pray "in his name" (John 16.24). But following Jesus and experiencing a deep intimacy with God should not cut us off from others; it should be an entrance into fuller and better knowledge of both them and ourselves.

Because Judaism is the cradle of Christianity in a very literal way, Christians ought to be able to be sensitive to and grateful for what we can receive from other religions. Such an open approach does not threaten the uniqueness of Jesus' vision of God or his teaching. Jesus did say, "no one comes to the Father except by me" (John 14.6), but only after he had already said, "in my Father's house are many mansions" (John 14.2). Various interpretations of these words are possible, but if we have been taught that Christianity is inclusive rather than exclusive then we may well come to see how Jesus' knowledge of God, which he so gladly shares with any who will hear, supplements and complements insights from other sources rather than rivals or contradicts them.

As we shall see, Ruth found the abiding presence of God through taking part in forms of worship other than the ones she had been brought up in. In our own time Mother Teresa prays daily with the Church and draws the strength she needs for her work, and then she serves the needs of all she meets without discrimination of any kind. Her "home for the dying" is a place where Hindus, Muslims, and Christians can die with dignity, having received the rituals of their own way of believing and faith.

MOTHER TERESA

One of Mother Teresa's favourite texts is from St Paul, "Yet not I, but Christ liveth in me" (Galatians 2.20). She has always refused to have a biography written about her. To one would-be enquirer, Malcom Muggeridge, she wrote back:

> *Christ's life was not written during his lifetime, yet he did the greatest work on earth – he redeemed the world and taught mankind to love his Father. The Work is his Work and to remain so, all of us are but his instruments, who do our little bit and pass by.*

Mother Teresa in effacing herself becomes herself, yet even so she does sometimes refer to her life story. Her home had been an exceptionally happy one. So when her vocation came to her as a schoolgirl, the only impediment was precisely this loving happy home which she did not wish to leave. In an interview about how her vocation came to her, she described her home in former Yugoslavia. She said it was:

> *In Skopje in Yugoslavia. I was only twelve years old then. I lived at home with my parents; we children used to go to a non-Catholic school but we also had very good priests who*

were helping the boys and girls to follow their vocation according to the call of God. It was then that I first knew I had a vocation to the poor, in 1922.

She became a nun and was sent to teach at the Loreto convent school in Calcutta, in India, work in most pleasant surroundings which she also thoroughly enjoyed. Then the second great break in Mother Teresa's life took place; the call within a call, as she puts it. She had occasion to go into some of the very poorest streets of Calcutta and suddenly realized that she belonged there, not in her Loreto convent with its pleasant garden, eager schoolgirls, congenial colleagues, and rewarding work.

To be released from her vows was a complicated and lengthy process. It took two years before she was free to go back into the world and then take stricter vows of her own devising. When at last she left her convent, she stepped out with a few rupees in her pocket, made her way to the poorest, wretchedest quarter of the city, found a lodging there, gathered together a few abandoned children – there were plenty to choose from – and began her ministry of love.

Other Sisters started coming to her in 1949. At first there were only 12 – that was in 1959 – but gradually the numbers kept on increasing. For ten years, says Mother Teresa, "we did not move out of Calcutta, because we had to train our Sisters for the work. In 1959, when we opened the first house in Dranchi and then one in Delhi, the numbers of Sisters started increasing and we began getting girls from the very places where we had opened houses."

Mother Teresa is fond of saying that what the poor need even more than food and clothing and shelter (though they need these too, desperately) is to be wanted. It is the outcast state their poverty imposes upon them that is most agonizing. She has a place in her heart for them all. To her, they are all children of God, for whom Christ died, and so deserving of all love. If God counts the hairs on each of their heads, if none are excluded from the salvation the death of Christ offers, who will venture to exclude them from earthly blessings and esteem?

Recently Mother Teresa has received some sharp criticism and her reputation as one of the great saints of our modern world has been questioned. Much of the criticism, however, misses the point – her work is solely a ministry of love. She expects to achieve nothing more than to be used by God to give a sign to anyone she can that his love is freely available to all. Death has been called the great leveller. For the dying all that matters is to know God's love. The other details of life – religion, class, status – are less important than knowing God's love for each and every person. By concentrating all her energy on such a relatively simple task, Mother Teresa is clearly used by God. Through her and her work his love has touched many people *in this world*, and God is glorified.

Here are testimonies from those who have seen Mother Teresa at work to her remarkable witness to Christ.

- I never experienced so perfect a sense of human equality as with Mother Teresa among her poor. Her love for them, reflecting God's love, makes them equal, as brothers and sisters within a family are equal, however widely they differ in intellectual and other attainments, in physical beauty and grace.

- To me one of the most wonderful things about your work is that you make one see that all these poor people are wonderful people, that these children are exquisite children, this and the fact that you have the principle that no one must ever be refused. That there is no qualification, no selectivity.

- When the train began to move, and I walked away, I felt as though I was leaving behind me all the beauty and all the joy in the universe. Something of God's universal love has rubbed off on Mother Teresa giving her homely features a noticeable luminosity; a shining quality.

And here are two prayers and a meditation written by Mother Teresa.

- Make us worthy, Lord, to serve our fellows throughout the world who live and die in poverty and hunger.

- Give them through our hands this day their daily bread, and by our understanding love, give peace and joy.

- The fruit of silence is prayer
  The fruit of prayer is faith
  The fruit of faith is love
  The fruit of love is service
  The fruit of service is peace.

In her famous interview for BBC TV in the 1970s, Malcom Muggeridge asked Mother Teresa, "The stimulus, the fire, the strength of what you're doing, where does it come from?" She replied, "It comes from Christ, without him we could do nothing, and in him we see that suffering can become a means to greater love, and greater generosity".

Each day Mother Teresa meets Jesus; first by receiving Holy Communion, where she draws strength from him who promised to be with us in the breaking of the bread; and then in each needing suffering soul she sees and tends. They are one and the same Jesus: in Holy Communion and in the streets. Both types of encounter are "sacraments" and neither exists without the other, and perceiving that unity is the strength of all praying.

RUTH

Most people have a particular fondness for the story of Ruth. "The loveliest little epic and idyllic whole that tradition has given us" is how Goethe once described it. In the Hebrew scriptures it comes in a different place in the sequence of books from its place in the Bible, because it was read as part of the Jewish liturgy for the feast of Pentecost – a kind of harvest festival which celebrated the wheat harvest.

Ruth is the prototype of the gentile who is welcomed and accepted into another religion, a religion which has tendencies to become exclusive rather than inclusive in its outlook and practice. The open welcome she received had significant results for both Judaism and Christianity. The book finishes like this:

> *Naomi took the child and laid him in her lap and became his nurse. Her neighbours gave him a name: "Naomi has a son," they said; "we will call him Obed." He was the father of Jesse, the father of David.*

Ruth 4.17

Ruth is one of the ancestors of Jesus. He already, if you like, contains within himself those of other nations and religions.

Moab was a small hilly country across the River Jordan on the other side of the Dead Sea. Naomi and her family left Bethlehem at a time when Judah was suffering drought and they found Moab was still fertile. While living there, her sons married local girls. Sadly, her husband and both her sons, Mahlon and Chilion, died and the women were left to fend for themselves.

The marriage laws which are mentioned (Ruth 4.7) appear to come from a time long before the book was actually written down, and so they require a certain amount of interpretation and explanation to Jews living in the fifth century BC. Marriage customs among the Jews directed that in order to preserve property and inherit-ance another member of the family should take over a dead husband's responsibilities. So Naomi decided to return to Bethlehem, but urged her two daughters-in-law to stay with their own people. One of them, Orpah, agreed but, in one of the most beautiful passages in the Bible, the other, Ruth, gently but firmly refused.

> *Ruth said, Entreat me not to leave you or to return from following you; for where you go I will go, and where you lodge I will lodge; your people shall be my people, and your God my God; where you die, I will die, and there will I be buried.*

Ruth 1.16–17

When they arrived back in Bethlehem, "at the beginning of barley harvest", Ruth was an immigrant and she worked in the fields as a gleaner following the reapers. The right of the poor to glean was part of Israel's rough and ready social security system (cf. Leviticus 19.9f). Boaz saw her and protected her, and accepted that she had a kinship with him even though strictly he need not have done so. His generosity proclaims a wideness in God's mercy which reveals the extent of the divine love.

Probably this short book was actually written as a parable (like Jonah, which comes from much the same period and has a similar message) to teach and illustrate certain truths about God which were being forgotten or ignored.

- The emphasis on Ruth's Moabite ancestry raises the question of how strictly the Jewish law should be applied. Should Judaism be exclusive and narrow, or should it be inclusive and provide within it space and a welcome for gentiles?

- The idyll of Ruth and Boaz – an ancient, often repeated story – reminded the ardent but narrow Jew that David, the ideal king as he had come to be regarded, was descended from a woman who was a Moabitess, but who had shown great piety in leaving her own people to join herself to her husband's people.

- The writer is concerned to show that any who accept God's protection, who "find shelter beneath his wings" (Ruth 2.12), can become members of his true and obedient people.

- We should see the story as designed to demonstrate the loving care and providence of God. The famine, the deaths, the desolation of the opening scene are shown nevertheless to be within the care of God. Out of a seemingly hopeless situation, he is working out for those who have faith in him a new assurance in the future. There is no superficial pretence that life is not hard; there is in such a situation the knowledge that "by turning everything to their good, God co-operates with all those who love him" (Romans 8.28).

Now look at two passages from the same period when the book was written and see just how narrow Judaism had become.

In the time of Ezra and Nehemiah (450–400 BC) the Jewish community had, by force of circumstances, become highly exclusive. There were rigorous, fanatical attempts to keep pure the great revelation they had received, and to prevent it being contaminated or diluted by the paganism of the nations around them. It was only too easy for this religious zeal to become arrogant and hostile to the gentiles.

> *Ezra the priest stood up and said to them, "You have trespassed and married foreign women, and so increased the guilt of Israel. Now then make confession to the Lord the God of your fathers, and do his will; separate yourselves from the peoples of the land and from foreign wives." Then all the assembly answered with a loud voice, "It is so; we must do as you have said".*

Ezra 10.10–12

> *In those days also I saw the Jews who had married women of Ashdod, Ammon and Moab; and half of their children spoke the language of Ashdod, and they could not speak the language of Judah, but the language of each people. And I contended with them and cursed them and beat some of them and pulled out their hair; and I made them take an oath in the name of God saying, "You shall not give your daughters for your sons or for yourselves. Did not Solomon king of Israel sin on account of such women? Among the many nations there was no king like him, and he was loved*

by God, and God made him king over all Israel; never-
theless foreign women made even him to sin. Shall we then
listen to you and do all this great evil and act treacherously
against our God by marrying foreign women?"

Nehemiah 13.23–27

Such passages make us very uncomfortable, especially at a time
when across Europe, particularly, many problems are coming to the
surface as people try to find ways of living with outsiders and with
"strangers in their midst". It is almost unbelievable to read such
violent words in scripture, which come so close to the appalling
violence which nowadays hides under the name of ethnic cleansing.

But compare that narrow, tunnel vision with the vision from an
earlier period in Jewish history and we see immediately how a
corrupt Judaism should be rejected.

It shall come to pass in the latter days
that the mountain of the house of the Lord
shall be established as the highest of the mountains,
and shall be raised above the hills;
and all the nations shall flow to it,
and many peoples shall come, and say:
"Come, let us go up to the mountain of the Lord
to the house of the God of Jacob;
that he may teach us his ways
and that we may walk in his paths."
For out of Zion shall go forth the law,
and the word of the Lord from Jerusalem.
He shall judge between the nations,
and shall decide for many peoples;
and they shall beat their swords into ploughshares,
and their spears into pruning hooks;
nation shall not lift up sword against nation,
neither shall they learn war any more.

Isaiah 2.2–4

The parable of Ruth is retold to recover the older, purer view of
God, and in order to bring home the truth that the God of Israel is
God of all the nations. Judaism must not degenerate into a dry
legalistic religion but be, as it always had been, a faith for all who
would know God, and a faith which brings all the nations within
his love and providence. Ruth's acceptance of this ancient vision of
God's love for all human beings is our example too.

READINGS

1. A world of many faiths

We live today in a world of unprecedented ethnic, social, cultural and religious pluralism; a situation which creates new opportunities and new problems for all of us. For centuries India has witnessed the coexistence of many different ethnic and religious groups. Hindus, Buddhists, Jains and Sikhs have India as their land of origin, but from an early age members of other religious communities came from the outside and settled here too. Christians, Parsis, Muslims and Jews – so that we find an extraordinary mosaic of faiths throughout the Indian subcontinent.

Today's global situation of religious pluralism should be seen as an important opportunity for mutual enrichment rather than for communal tension. We must explore together the specific insights, the moments of revelation and disclosure, the spiritual treasures which our respective faiths have accumulated and handed down from generation to generation, whereby the lives of countless people have been nourished, sustained and transformed; today as in the past. If we are honest with each other, as we must be, we will recognise our profound diversities in belief and practice, and this can be a deeply painful experience. There are not only differences between our various religions, but there also exists pluralism within each of our own communities of faith. There are different kinds of Hinduism, of Buddhism, of Jainism, Islam, Sikhism, and so on, just as there are many different historical and theological strands within Christianity. Yet we recognise today that each faith possesses an irreplaceable spiritual heritage, a specific message and distinctive identity of its own which is of tremendous importance for all of us.

Robert Runcie, Address to leaders of many faiths at
Bishop's House, Calcutta, 13 February 1986

2.   Who are the missionaries now?

*It wasn't long ago that you got on a P & O boat to see a
Buddhist. You went to the Middle East to see a Muslim.
You went to India to see a Hindu. Sikhism was for the
Sikhs in the Punjab. Shintoism was for the Japanese, who
were not to be found anywhere near South Wales or
Middlesborough. But in 1985 there were 5 million
Muslims in Europe; 2 million of them in France.
Practitioners of yoga and zen abound, and not only on
the wilder shores of California. At the same time,
Christianity, in one of its Westernised forms, exists in the
heartlands of Hinduism, Buddhism and Islam.*

Eric James, *Judge Not*, p. 103

3.   Paths to God

*I believe that God not only invites all people to find
their wholeness and freedom in a relationship with
himself, but that he also guides them from the place
where they are. The starting point for each person will
be what, through his response to the religious and
cultural influences which have moulded him, he has
become. I believe God leads the vast majority of
Hindus by a Hindu path and of Muslims by a Muslim
one. I do not believe that all religions are equally true
or helpful to their adherents, any more than I believe
that all cultures are equally rich or that all people are
equally wise. Nor do I rule out God's drawing a
person to transfer allegiance from one faith to
another. Indeed in the ecumenical climate of today and
the growing respect and friendliness between the
adherents of different religions this is likely to happen
more frequently in the future than in the past. But
these will be the exceptions; and I believe that God
draws the great majority of men and women to find
their way to him within the religion in which they have
grown up.*

Christopher Bryant, *The Heart in Pilgrimage*

4. A seed of tolerance

3rd February

To Oxford to interview George Appleton, once the Anglican Archbishop in Jerusalem. A lovable and holy old chap who is not afraid of a spot of heresy. When I asked if it were possible to convince Muslims that Christians really did worship one God and not three, he said, "Well, I'm not at all sure of that myself." After a distinctly universalist passage I asked, "But surely you believe that Christianity is in some sense the best religion?" To which he replied "Yes – for Christians." Which is exactly right.

Gerald Priestland, Diary

5. Open or shut doors

Religions separate men and women from one another and tempt them to boast of what they possess and others do not; the Gospel is the proclamation that they already belong together as children of the one God and Father of all, and the Church is the Kingdom or Family in which their unity is to be realised.

Alec Vidler, *Soundings*, p. 242

6. Put to new use

I went to the municipality and I asked them to give me a place where I could bring these people because on the same day I had found other people dying in the streets. The health officer of the municipality took me to the temple, the Kali Temple, and showed me the dormashalah where the people used to rest after they had done their worship of Kali goddess. It was an empty building; he asked me if I would accept it. I was very happy to have that place for many reasons, but especially knowing that it was a centre of worship and devotion of the Hindus. Within twenty-four hours we had our patients there and we started the work of the home for the sick and dying who are destitutes. Since then we have picked up over twenty-three thousand people from the streets of Calcutta of which about fifty per cent have died.

Mother Teresa, BBC interview

7. To see Christ in one another

From the day they join the community we spend a very good deal of time in training the Sisters, especially in the spirit and the life of the society which is beautifully defined in the constitution. This is the written will of God for us. Also, side by side with the spiritual training, they have to go to the slums. Slum work and this meeting with the people is a part of the noviciate training. This is something special to us as a congregation because as a rule novices do not go out, but to be able to understand the meaning of our fourth vow, which promises that we give out wholehearted free service to the poorest of the poor – to Christ in his distressing disguise – because of this it is necessary that they come face to face with the reality, so as to be able to understand what their life is going to be, when they will have taken their vows and when they will have to meet Christ twenty-four hours a day in the poorest of the poor in the slums.

We must be able to radiate the joy of Christ, express it in our actions. If our actions are just useful actions that give no joy to the people, our poor people would never be able to rise up to the call which we want them to hear, the call to come closer to God. We want to make them feel they are loved. If we went to them with a sad face, we would only, make them much more depressed.

Mother Teresa, BBC interview

PRAYERS

1. Adoration

> And the foreigners who join themselves to the Lord,
> to minister to him, to love the name of the Lord, and to
>   be his servants,
> everyone who keeps the sabbath, and does not
>   profane it, and holds fast my covenant –
> these I will bring to my holy mountain, and make them
> joyful in my house of prayer;
> their burnt offerings and their sacrifices
> will be accepted at my alter;
> for my house shall be called a house of prayer
>   for all peoples.

Isaish 56.6, 7

Give thanks to God for this vision of all people brought to his kind and gentle rule and made together into one family.

2. Penitence

> Has this house, which is called by my name, become a den of robbers in your eyes? Behold, I myself have seen it, says the Lord.

Jeremiah 7.11

Look at the times when your discipleship and your prayers have been too narrow and exclusive, keeping others out instead of welcoming them in, and ask God to heal and forgive.

3.   Intercession

"I am the Lord, the God of Abraham your father and the God of Isaac; the land on which you lie I will give to you and to your descendants; and your descendants shall be like the dust of the earth, and you shall spread abroad to the west and to the east and to the north and to the south; and by you and your descendants shall all the families of the earth bless themselves."

Genesis 28.13, 14

Give thanks for all that God has revealed of himself through prophets and seekers of many faiths; and pray for everyone who seeks truths with integrity, that God will bring us all to himself, so that we may grow together knowing both his correction and fulfilment.

4.   Dedication

Arise, shine; for your light has come,
and the glory of the Lord has risen upon you.
For behold, darkness shall cover the earth,
and thick drakness the peoples;
but the Lord will arise upon you,
and his glory will be seen upon you.
And nations shall come to your light,
and kings to the brightness of your rising.

Isaiah 60.1–3

Ask God to keep you faithful to the insights he gives and to the truth which he has invited you to share, and pray that he may use such light to draw others to himself.

5.   Written Prayers

O God, I gaze in wonder at thy creative love;
at thy seeking for people everywhere
and their search for thee,
showing thyself in ways they can understand.
Help me to learn more of thee from the experience of
   other communities of faith,
and so to live and love that others may learn to share
   what I have found of thee in Jesus Christ.
Open my eyes; enlighten my mind; enlarge my heart;
and grant that my own expression of thee in life and
   word
may come closer to thy eternal truth and love: O God,
   my God, God of all.

Bishop George Appleton

Word of God and Light of mankind, we ask you to
bless all those of other faiths with whom we share
our lives and who serve the needs of our community.
Help us to discern in them the light that lightens all
people and to love them with a love like yours; that
as we join with them in service of others we may be
drawn closer to you, the Way, the Truth and the
Life. Amen

God and Father of all, who made of one blood all the
   nations of the earth: deepen our understandings of
   peoples of other races, religions and languages than
   our own.
Teach us to see them in the light of your own
   all-embracing love and creative purpose; and give us
   a vision of the true brotherhood of mankind, united
   into one family.
We ask this in the name of him who died that all might
   be saved, even Jesus Christ our Lord. Amen

5 CANDLE IN THE WIND
AFFLICTION

INTRODUCTION

The time of tension between dying and birth (T.S. Eliot)

Christopher Bryant in his book, *The Heart in Pilgrimage*, writes: "Prayer not only reaches up to heaven, but it also sounds the murky depths of our nature and the dark energies of earth." Fifty years after the end of the Second World War we are still confronting both the depths of human nature and the evil of the world in terrible and agonizing ways. Today, as I am writing, it is the anniversary of the week-long fire-storm over Dresden, while a month ago it was the anniversary of the opening of the concentration camp at Auschwitz. Whether the twentieth century has brought greater evil than other centuries is rather a vain question. We must accept, though, that it continues to raise with great intensity the unending conflict between God's goodness and the reality of evil, a struggle which always engulfs us.

I no longer believe, if I ever did, there is an "answer" to the "problem of suffering". The traditional way of putting the question is profoundly unhelpful. Suffering is experienced and can only be handled from the interior, not intellectualized and discussed as a topic. When Jesus teaches about suffering, he deliberately uses the images of baptism, being immersed in something, and childbirth with the labour every mother has to undergo. In a word, in whatever form suffering comes it has to be prayed through before it can be handled, let alone explained. Those who say the most useful things about suffering will seem tentative and reticent, but they always speak from personal experience, as did both Solzhenitsyn and Jeremiah.

However and whenever we experience any aspect of human suffering, then, we should look hard to see not just that within its pain and destructiveness God is present, but also how he is actually *at work* – working to bring his sovereign rule to bear on his creation. The divine activity is as vital as the divine presence. In praying through affliction we shall find at least three things happening which bring us into that action: (a) we will be going further into the darkness of the world; (b) we will be learning how to stand and bear it and "having done all to stand" (Ephesians 6.13); and (c) we shall discover how to turn affliction into intercession.

A first hint of the depth and demand of this part of praying often comes when we face what the guides in prayer call aridity.

> *The man who after his first steps in the spiritual life, throws himself into the struggle of prayer and union with God, is astounded at the dryness of the road.*

> *The more he advances, the more the darkness thickens around him. The more he goes on, the more bitter and insipid everything becomes. He derives little comfort from the recollection of times past when God seemed to make his spiritual path easier.*

> *Sometimes he is even tempted to shout, "But Lord, if you helped a little more, more people would follow you."*

Carlo Carretto, Letters from the Desert

God was in Christ reconciling the world to himself (2 Corinthians 5.19)

Attempting to pray within suffering faces us with more than dryness. Immediately we confront another aspect of the pain and anguish – our own impotence and nothingness. We do not have any power of ourselves to help ourselves, as the old collect put it.

On the one hand, anyone with a shred of sensitivity is overwhelmed by the pain of the world which comes to us. On the other, we are reduced to nothing when we realize how little we can ever do to help, which makes the pain more intense and searing. Caught between the longing to help and our inability to help, our confidence goes, our belief in the power of prayer evaporates, and we turn in other directions to take our mind off such things just to keep going. Diversion tactics are entirely understandable. Drawing attention to them is not intended to make us feel guilty, but instead to invite us to go deeper into the darkness and through it to find out exactly what it is, in Christ, that we can do.

Read again Mark 9.1–29. In this passage the contrast between vision and frustration, between the mountain top and impotence in praying, is very clear. After Jesus had taken three of the disciples to a place of exalted prayer, on their return they met the failure of the other disciples who were completely unable to heal an epileptic boy. This need not imply that Peter, James, and John, who had been with Jesus, would have done any better. That is not the point. The disciples who were among the crowds and to whom the father brought his son in the agony of his need were unable to do the work of the kingdom and to heal the boy. "Why could we not cast it out?" the disciples asked Jesus when they were alone with him after he had healed the boy. He said, "There is no means of casting out this sort but prayer."

The chapter starts with Jesus' promise that some of those standing there would not see death before they had seen the Kingdom of God already come in power (Mark 9.1). So Mark is telling us that *both incidents* – the vision of the transfiguration and the healing of the boy – display the Kingdom of God, present in its full power.

Bishop Michael Ramsey used to insist that the journey Jesus makes to the Father is a single journey, which takes him to heaven and into the darkness of the world at the same time. Here is where the cost of discipleship is at its greatest, for Jesus and for his friends. This is the moment when everything about our praying crumbles and falls away, however much we struggle to reassemble the bits. Towards the end of his life Cardinal Newman, wrote "as the years go on, I have less and less sensible devotion and inward life". When that happens to us we have reached the point where St Paul appeals that having done all, *we must still stand* (Ephesians 6.10–18). Standing at this point is the place to find the links between the promised glory of the creation, its disordering by evil and sin, and its longing for renewal and fulfilment, and discover how God brings together and unifies them in praying.

Standing at the point of intercession

Now here is an answer – not an answer to the problem of suffering but an answer to the question, what can be done about it through praying? Adoration leads us through the collapse of any power of self-help we can draw on to the recognition of our true need, which is to acknowledge our total dependance on God; which in turn leads us to intercession. This is the place where the work of prayer takes over.

Look again at Jesus and his understanding of his own prayers as he goes through suffering and death. Jesus used the Scriptures to interpret his vocation and how it was being worked out. We don't often picture Jesus himself using the Bible, but clearly he did and in Isaiah 53.4–5, he read, as we do, a description of the suffering of the servant of God and how his suffering achieved healing.

> *Yet on himself he bore our sufferings,*
> *our torments he endured,*
> *while we counted him smitten by God,*
> *struck down by disease and misery;*
> *but he was pierced for our transgressions;*
> *tortured for our iniquities;*
> *the chastisement he bore is health for us*
> *and by his scourging we are healed.*

We have no record that Jesus believed he was acting out these words in his suffering, and many scholars say he did not identify himself with the suffering servant of God. His teaching was not centred on what he is doing so much as on what God is doing, but it is perfectly easy to see how God was fulfilling the words of Isaiah in Jesus' ministry. Jesus went through all that was demanded of him, certain that in his Father's hands intercession for others in their deepest need is an instrument for the salvation and the healing of the world.

Probably we know more of affliction than any other generation of Christians, partly because of modern means of communication but also because of modern knowledge about ourselves in the depth of our psychology. "This knowledge" writes Mother Mary Clare, "must be redirected into and held by the conscious prayer of those who are channels of God's redemptive love – which is the real essence of intercessory prayer".

Mother Mary Clare lived in Oxford at Fairacres with the Sisters of the Love of God. It was during the 1941 Cardiff blitz when she suffered from insomnia that she came to realize her distinctive vocation which was to pray, particularly in the night – the pray of intercessory, reparatory, contemplation.

> *He who prays*
> *stands at that point*
> *of intercession*
> *where the love of God*
> *and the tensions and*
> *sufferings we inflict*
> *on each other*
> *meet and are held*
> *to the healing power of God.*

In affliction God himself is suffering and he invites us to bear it with him, a task for which he also promises to provide the required strength. Here prayer for others and for ourselves goes on ceaselessly day and night, which is the silent dynamo working and bringing God's kingdom among us.

ALEXANDER SOLZHENITSYN

Alexander Solzhenitsyn is a survivor. Three times he has looked at death face to face: in the Second World War; during years in detention in the notorious prison camps in Siberia; and when he was told he had an inoperable cancer. Yet it is not this personal suffering and heroism for which he is so famous. His Nobel Prize in 1970 was for literature. It is Solzhenitsyn's voice, heard by the world through his writings and speeches, which has made him famous. Solzhenitsyn draws on two main sources for his writing, his own experiences in prison and his deep Russian Orthodox faith. The writing is part of a long tradition in denunciatory Russian literature which many would call prophetic.

When he lived in America, ironically, he was dismissed as a jeremiad, a prophet of gloom and doom. There are several parallels in experience and faith between Solzhenitsyn and Jeremiah, both suffering in mind and spirit and body because of their conviction that they have to be prophets to the nations. The message of each of these two men comes from an inner life of enormous power and integrity. Both were abused and put in prison because their message was unacceptable to the politicians and rulers of the day. Both reveal their sensitivity and courage by the inventiveness of their imagination, and both invite us to suffer for the truth's sake and to trust in God.

Solzhenitsyn was born in December 1918, six months after his father had been killed accidentally while serving in the army as an artillery officer. He grew up in considerable hardship during the 1920s and 1930s in Rostov-on-Don. He had wanted to be a writer when he left school, but finding he couldn't begin such a career at the time, he took a degree in mathematics at his local university and completed a correspondence course in literature instead. He married in 1940 and went into the Russian army in October 1941, serving throughout the Second World War and twice being decorated for bravery.

As the war came to an end in 1945, he was arrested for having made disrespectful remarks about Stalin in private correspondence. He was sent back to Moscow where he was interrogated, tried, and sentenced to eight years' imprisonment, followed by what was called "perpetual exile". He was held in various camps, including one which became the setting for his first published novel *One Day in the Life of Ivan Denisovich*.

He was released from prison in 1953, after the death of Stalin. But by now he had contracted cancer and he went to the Tashkent clinic where unexpectedly he recovered. He was not released from "perpetual exile" though until 1956, when he went to live near Vladamir where he was visited by his wife. They had divorced previously but now they agreed to remarry.

The publication of *One Day in the Life of Ivan Denisovich* in 1962 became a political event of real magnitude. It gave an explicit picture of life in Stalin's slave-labour camps and broke open the truth about Stalinism which the authorities found less and less easy to accept, and which would in the end help to destroy the system itself. Although Solzhenitsyn became famous overnight and was publicly praised by Krushchev, his outspoken criticism of the Soviet establishment proved too much. His plays and books were prohibited and, when he was awarded the Nobel prize for literature in 1970, a campaign of vilification was launched against him. In spite of this, he allowed Parts I and II of the *Gulag Archipelago* to be published outside the Soviet Union in 1973. This increased the attacks on him and his associates because it described so clearly the truth about the camps, and the ruthlessness and hypocrisy of Communism. In 1974 he was again arrested, stripped, interrogated and sent into exile; this time to the West, taking up residence in Zurich in Switzerland where he was joined by his second wife and three sons.

Solzhenitsyn's residence in the West, however, did not turn out to be as easy as might have been expected. He did not fit into society in the West any more than in the East. When he moved to the USA, his vociferous opposition to Western life and politics was as uncompromising as his opposition to Communism. The speech he made at Harvard University when he was made an honorary doctor of letters in June 1978 was a denunciation of the West's abrogation of Christian responsibilities and its spiritual bankruptcy. When he was interviewed by a Czech journalist Pavel Licko about his controversial play *Candle in the Wind* he said, "I wanted to point out the moral problems of society in technically developed countries, irrespective of whether they are capitalist or socialist".

Russian citizenship was restored to Solzhenitsyn in 1990 and he timed his moment to return carefully. First, though, he wrote a long essay "How do we rebuild Russia?" which was published in two Moscow papers in 1990 and many believe the essay had a great influence on President Boris Yeltsin. Solzhenitsyn, however, waited until 27 May 1994 to return home, 20 years after being bundled into exile and 75 years old. But it quickly became apparent that he had returned too late to do anything effective for the new Russia in spite of receiving a rapturous welcome. He soon launched a stinging criticism against the unbridled capitalism which had replaced Communism. His denunciations were expressed with such sharp clarity that the new rulers were still uncomfortable with this prophetic voice and uncertain they could support this man from the past.

In *One Day in the Life of Ivan Denisovich*, Shukhov says the first law is "Thou shalt survive" and the second is "but not at the expense of your fellow-sufferer". Like Solzhenitsyn himself, he not merely survived his ordeals but survived them with his moral values and integrity intact. The same moral power is the source of Solzhenitsyn's criticism of society. His speech when he received the Nobel prize for literature in 1970 was based on a Russian proverb, "One word of truth shall outweigh the whole world". For Solzhenitsyn, truth is the only adequate foundation for heroism. He stands as a candle in the wind, unremittingly proclaiming the truth as he sees it, with the power, imagination, and spirituality of a Christian prophet, as well as the unique talent of a great Russian writer.

JEREMIAH

> *We make of our quarrel with others, rhetoric;*
> *we make of our quarrel with ourselves, poetry.*

> W. B. Yeats

The second part of Yeats's observation certainly applies to Jeremiah. He wrote many passages of poetry, most of it introspective and full of inner agony. Like Solzhenitsyn, it is from his writings that we can know the man. He has left us some of the most intimate and self-revelatory passages in the Bible. His affliction as a prophet seems to have gone deeper than the personal suffering of other prophets. He was torn apart by his wish to be

faithful to his vocation on the one hand and his natural reticence on
the other. His mood swings are obvious and register deeply. Many
suffer the same extremes of confidence and humiliation and move
between them, like Jeremiah, in their journey of faith and in
their praying.

Jeremiah can rejoice in his task. He knows God upholds him and
will save him.

> *The Lord said,... you shall go to whatever people I send*
> *you and say whatever I tell you to say. Fear none of them,*
> *for I am with you and will keep you safe.*

Jeremiah 1.7–8

> *But the Lord is on my side, strong and ruthless,*
> *therefore my persecutors shall stumble and fall powerless.*
> *Bitter shall be their abasement when they fall,*
> *and their shame shall long be remembered.*
> *O Lord of Hosts, thou dost test the righteous*
> *and search the depths of the heart;*
> *to thee have I committed my cause,*
> *let me see thee take vengeance on them.*
> *Sing to the Lord, praise the Lord;*
> *for he rescues the poor from those who would do them wrong.*

Jeremiah 20.11–13

But Jeremiah also knows that his message will be rejected. In
addition in many painful ways he himself, the messenger, will be
rejected as well. Jeremiah's affliction includes imprisonment,
being put in the stocks, and thrown into a cistern. The agony within
him is so extreme that at times he wishes he had never been born,
and his spiritual experience of God can be so bleak that his praying
becomes almost impossible. He calls God a dried-up spring with
no longer any refreshment or water in it.

> *Alas, alas, my mother, that you ever gave me birth!*
> *a man doomed to strife, with the whole world against me.*
> *I have borrowed from no one, I have lent to no one,*
>   *yet all men abuse me.*
>
>   *Lord, thou knowest;*
> *remember me, Lord, and come to visit me,*
> *take vengeance for me on my persecutors.*
>   *Be patient with me and take me not away,*
> *see what reproaches I endure for thy sake.*

> *I have to suffer those who despise thy words,*
> *but thy word is joy and happiness to me,*
>   *for thou hast named me thine,*
>   *O Lord, God of Hosts.*
>
> *I have never kept company with any gang of roisterers,*
>   *or made merry with them;*
> *because I felt thy hand upon me I have sat alone;*
>   *for thou hast filled me with indignation.*
>
> *Why then is my pain unending,*
>   *my wound desperate and incurable?*
> *Thou art to me like a brook that is not to be trusted,*
>   *whose waters fail.*

Jeremiah 15.10, 15–18

The other autobiographical poems in the series are
10.23–24; 11.18—12.6; 17.9–10, 14–18; 18.18–23;
20.7–12, 14–18. They have been called by some people
"Confessions", but this is not quite the right description because they are more like prayer; a deeply personal dialogue
between Jeremiah and his Lord.

Jeremiah may have been born about 626 BC and was probably still
alive in 570 BC living in Egypt where, tradition says, he was
eventually stoned to death by his fellow countrymen. He was born
in the village of Anathoth, two miles north-east of Jerusalem. The
capital was about an hour's walk away, and he spent his adult
years in the city and at its royal court. His writings reveal how well
he knew both the countryside and city life.

He lived through great upheavals which were taking place
in world affairs and in the history of his own nation. The
Assyrian Empire which had been set up in the eighth century was
fast coming to an end. While one great nation was crumbling
and before another had taken its place, King Josiah of Judah
(640–609 BC) was able to strike a blow for religious and political
independence for his small kingdom. Josiah used the opportunity
to good effect. He put into practice religious reforms based
on the text of a book found by accident in the temple, which

was probably the original text of Deuteronomy. Then for a time it looked as though Egypt would inherit the influence and power of Assyria. In the end, though, it was Babylon which took its place and dominated world affairs.

Josiah was succeeded by two of his sons. The first one only survived for a few months. The second one, Jehoiakim, was a puppet king of both Egypt and Babylon. He died during the famous siege of Jerusalem in 598 BC which led to the destruction of his kingdom. Many Jews were then deported from Judah to Babylon and another puppet king, Zedekiah, ruled.

While his country was being threatened and invaded by the terrible Babylonians, Jeremiah urged surrender as a religious duty – and did so consistently, whether in palace or prison. Jeremiah was the climax of a succession of prophets who dared to speak on behalf of Yahweh *against* Israel, warning them of judgement because of their apostasy. He became unacceptable to his people who denounced him and wanted him removed.

Tell this to the people of Jacob,
  proclaim it in Judah:
Listen, you foolish and senseless people,
who have eyes and see nothing,
ears and hear nothing.
Have you no fear of me? says the Lord;
will you not shiver before me,
  before me,
who made the shivering sand to bound the sea,
a barrier it never can pass?
Its waves heave and toss but they are powerless;
roar as they may, they cannot pass.
But this people has a rebellious and defiant heart,
rebels they have been and now they are clean gone.
They did not say to themselves,
"Let us fear the Lord our God,
who gives us the rains of autumn
and spring showers in their turn,
who brings us unfailingly
fixed seasons of harvest."
But your wrongdoing has upset nature's order;
and your sins have kept from you her kindly gifts.

An appalling thing, an outrage,
has appeared in this land:
prophets prophesy lies and priests go hand in hand with them,
and my people love to have it so.
How will you fare at the end of it all?

Jeremiah 5.20–25, 30–31

During any period of political instability, many political judgements will prove to be ill-founded and mistaken, and they are likely to arouse suspicion and hostility. Although Jeremiah's grasp of political power and reality was open to fierce criticism, he reached it because he believed God is Lord of the nations. He saw God's hand acting unmistakably within the events of history, and he believed God's people needed to accept whatever divine judgement came through world events which were ultimately under his control.

It was much the same conflict as the Church in the UK has lived with in the last twenty years. Politicians say they want the Church to stay out of politics, but the Church knows it has a message which must be proclaimed fearlessly even when it cuts at the heart and stability of the nation's life. If it is a message from God, arrived at through prayer and self-giving and self-criticism, then whether it is rejected and breeds hostility or not Christians must proclaim it.

The sustained attack which Jeremiah delivered on his own city before it fell to the Babylonians constitutes the most deeply moving example of the Israelite capacity for self-criticism. To most of those who first heard it, it was treachery. But to later generations, Jeremiah's prophecy was nothing less than the Word of God. In 605 BC Jeremiah dictated his prophecies to make a scroll, written by his faithful secretary Baruch. The scroll was read by a courtier named Jehudi to King Jehoiakim in his winter apartments with the fire burning in a brazier in front of him.

When Jehudi had read three or four columns of the scroll,
the king cut them off with a penknife and threw them into
the fire in the brazier. He went on doing so until the whole
scroll had been thrown on the fire... but the word of
Yahweh came to Jeremiah: now take another scroll and
write on it all the words that were on the first scroll which
Jehoiakim king of Judah burnt.

Jeremiah 36.23, 28

Imprisonment and rejection are often the cost of prophecy and prayer, but for Jeremiah it was only the beginning. The most poignant aspect of his despair of his people and nation is that it led him to despair of himself. His self-questioning inflicted great pain and brokenness within him, and in his praying he complained and questioned God:

> *O Lord, thou hast duped me, and I have been thy dupe;*
> * thou hast outwitted me and hast prevailed.*
> *I have been made a laughing-stock all the day long,*
> *everyone mocks me.*

Jeremiah 20.7

> *Deep within me my heart is broken,*
> *there is no strength in my bones;*
> *because of the Lord, because of his dread words*
> *I have become like a drunken man,*
> *like a man overcome with wine.*

Jeremiah 23.9

Jeremiah's prayers were often hard to bear, but after Jersualem had been set on fire and the population decimated by deportation, his words were still treasured and recalled – not only because their warnings had come true, but also because they pointed to one remaining hope. In chapter 37 the story is told of how during the last terrible days of the kingdom of Judah, Jeremiah bought a field near his ancestral village, Anathoth. It was a sign that houses, fields, vineyards would again be bought and sold in the land. But any hope of such restoration had to come by the action of God, not through political manoeuvres:

> *Listen to the word of the Lord, you nations,*
> *announce it, make it known to coasts and islands far away:*
> *He who scattered Israel shall gather them again*
> *and watch over them as a shepherd watches his flock.*
> *For the Lord has ransomed Jacob*
> *and redeemed him from a foe too strong for him.*
> *They shall come with shouts of joy to Zion's height,*
> *shining with happiness at the bounty of the Lord,*
> *the corn, the wine, and the oil,*
> *the young of flock and herd.*

Jeremiah 31.10–12

*The time is coming, says the Lord, when I will make a
new covenant with Israel and Judah. It will not be like
the covenant I made with their forefathers when I took
them by the hand and led them out of Egypt. Although
they broke my covenant, I was patient with them, says the
Lord. But this is the covenant which I will make with
Israel after those days, says the Lord; I will set my law
within them and write it on their hearts; I will become
their God and they shall become my people. No longer
need they teach one another to know the Lord; All of
them, high and low alike, shall know me, says the Lord,
for I will forgive their wrongdoing and remember their
sin no more.*

Jeremiah 33.31–34

READINGS

1. Purification

*Then the real battle begins and becomes serious. We are
beginning to discover what we are worth: nothing or little.
At earlier stages we thought we were generous; we now
discover that we are egoists. We thought, under the false
light of religious aestheticism, that we knew how to pray;
now we find that we no longer know how to say "Father".
We were convinced that we were humble, charitable,
obedient; now we find that pride has invaded our whole
being, down to the deepest roots. Prayer, human
relationships, working to spread the Gospel, all these seem
thwarted.*

*But we must render our accounts, and these are very poor.
With the exception of those privileged souls who
understood right from the beginning what the problem
really was, and who immediately set out upon the true,
rough road of humility and spiritual childhood, the greater
part of mankind is called upon to undergo a hard and
painful experience.*

Carlo Carretto, *Letters from the Desert*, p. 65

2. Intercession

*According to the Eastern tradition, it is not so much by
his teaching, nor even by his example that the spiritual
father helps his children, but rather by his prayer. The
father, in the image of Christ, must take upon himself
the trials, the imperfections and even the sins of those he
guides; he must expiate them and hold them before God
in prayer.*

A Carthusian, *The Way of Silent Love*

3. The work of praying

*It was told of abbot John the Dwarf that once he had
said to his elder brother: I want to live in the same
security as the angels have, doing no work, but serving
God without intermission. And casting off everything he
had on, he started out into the desert. When a week had
gone by he returned to his brother. And while he was
knocking on the door, his brother called out before
opening, and asked: Who are you? He replied: I am
John. Then his brother answered and said: John has
become an angel and is no longer among men. But John
kept on knocking and said: It is I. Still the brother did
not open, but kept him waiting. Finally, opening the
door, he said: John, angels who serve God unceasingly
do not need cells; but if you are a man, come and take up
the long work of prayer, labour and repentance. So John
did penance and said: Forgive me, brother, for I have
sinned.*

Thomas Merton, *The Wisdom of the Desert*

4. Confronting evil

*A simplistic view of evil in any situation that confronts us
is no longer an option for the Christian. As we say in
English, there are no "goodies" and "baddies". There*

are no absolute villains and no absolute heroes. None is absolutely innocent or absolutely guilty. The watchword of Christian faith – "no distinction, no discrimination", which is rooted in the way Jesus himself treated people, and which we welcome when it is applied to race and colour, or to men and women – that central watch- word has to be applied also to our judgement of the good and the bad in every situation of conflict. "There is no distinction", says Paul to the Romans, "for all alike have sinned". This does not absolve us from the conflict. We still know who are the people and what are the structures against which we have to contend. But we shall actually fight more effectively through recognising in ourselves as well as in those others the things we are fighting against. We shall be armed with new weapons through understanding in our own experience how the evil attitudes and the commit- ment to injustice took root. We shall discern more accurately the target for our attack when we see that we are not fighting flesh and blood, but ancient evil in the very fabric of earth and heaven.

John V. Taylor, *Weep Not for Me*

5. *To awaken hope*

It is this revelation of the vulnerability of God (in Jesus on the cross) that enables the Christian to hold on to his conviction of God's utter trustworthiness without shutting his eyes to life's tragic dimension. For if the gospel is to be indeed good news it must come as a message of healing and deliverance to man in his lostness, his compulsive hatred of and cruelty to himself and his fellows, his loneliness, his depression, his frustration, and all the many forms which human misery can take. It is because God has identified himself with man by undergoing something like the worst that could happen that he is able to persuade those who have strayed furthest from their true goal of the possibility of redemption and so awaken hope. Only those who have plumbed profoundly the depths of man's estrangement are able fully to grasp the hope of life beyond life which Christ's resurrection promises.

Christopher Bryant, *The Heart in Pilgrimage*

6. At one with affliction

We are tempted to forsake Christ and flee, concocting for our flight the most convincing reasons possible. We cannot bear to put ourselves in the same class as the afflicted. Yet this is also the road to resurrection, to fuller, richer life. For it is our hatred of what is buried within us, our fear of it and guilt about it, which keeps it excluded from our awareness. And it is precisely this exclusion which maintains it as an enemy felt to be working against us. When received into awareness, it loses its power to hurt or destroy, and, in time, contributes positively to the well-being and depth of the personality.

H. A. Williams, "Theology and self-awareness", in *Soundings*, p. 74

PRAYERS

1. Adoration

The soul has to go on loving in the emptiness, or at least to go on wanting to love, though it may be only with an infinitesimal part of itself. Then, one day, God will come to show himself to this soul and to reveal the beauty of the world to it.

Simone Weil, *Waiting on God*

Ask God to help you go far into yourself and your own feelings of hurt and pain, and the longing to be loved, and then look for the even stronger desire to love.

2. *Penitence*

Affliction makes God appear to be absent for a time, more absent than a dead man, more absent than light in the utter darkness of a cell. A kind of horror submerges the whole soul. During this absence there is nothing to love. What is terrible is that if, in this darkness where there is nothing to love, the soul ceases to love, God's absence becomes final.

Simone Weil, *Waiting on God*

Be brave and honest and indentify the times when you have given in to the force of darkness and stopped loving, and been unable to be with God. Then look for God in the darkness and ask for forgiveness.

3. *Intercession*

In true love it is not we who love the afflicted in God, it is God in us who loves them. When we are in affliction, it is God in us who loves those who wish us well. Compassion and gratitude come down from God, and when they are exchanged in a glance, God is present at the point where the eyes of those who give and those who receive meet.

Simone Weil, *Waiting on God*

Pray for those you know who are held tight in the grip of suffering and then try to hear them praying for you.

4. Dedication

Affliction, which means physical pain, distress of soul and social degradation, all at the same time, constitutes a nail. Yet a person whose soul remains ever turned in the direction of God while the nail pierces it, finds himself nailed to the very centre of the universe.

Simone Weil, *Waiting on God*

Christians promise to be with Jesus to the full, to the extent of being with him while he is dying on the cross. Try to understand more of what it means to be alongside him bearing the pain and sorrow of the world; and ask God to raise you, in his time and in his way, from such a place into the joy of his kingdom.

5. Written Prayers

Lord Jesus, by the loneliness of your suffering on the cross be near to all who are desolate and in pain or sorrow this day. May your presence transform their sorrow into comfort, and in fellowship with you may they find peace, for your mercy's sake. Amen

For those in need, O Lord, we make our prayer: the sick in mind or body, the blind and the deaf, the fatherless and the widow, the anxious and the perplexed, the sorrowing and the dying.
Give them courage, patience, and peace of heart, and do for them all that is for their good; for the sake of Jesus Christ our Lord. Amen

O Saviour of the world, who by thy cross and precious blood hast redeemed us: save us, and help us, we humbly beseech thee, O Lord.

*Thanks be to you, our Lord Jesus Christ, for all the
benefits which you have given us, for all the pains
and insults which you have borne for us.
Most merciful Redeemer, Friend and Brother, may we
know you more clearly, love you more dearly, and
follow you more nearly, day by day. Amen*

St Richard of Chichester 1197–1253

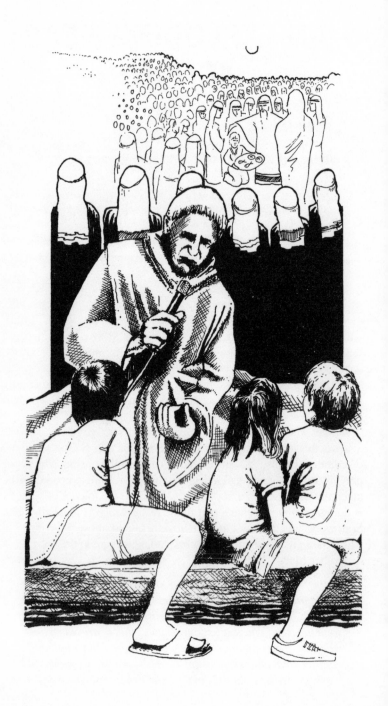

6 AN EXPLODING HEART
ACTION

INTRODUCTION

Our life is hid with Christ in God (Colossians 3.3)

Most of us want our praying to have an outcome, to be practical we might say, though put like that makes it sound wrong. We realize we have to train ourselves not to look for results, and above all not to measure the value of prayer by results or the lack of them. Yet the natural instinct that if it is worth doing something will happen cannot be left unexplored.

The fundamental action of praying is self-giving, and in every way it is all-giving with no motive of getting. But then Jesus tells us very clearly, "Ask, and you will receive; seek, and you will find; knock and the door will be opened" (Luke 11.9–10). So the wish to see the working out of prayer is well worth investigating – on one condition. We need to be absolutely convinced that praying is action, not a preliminary, or a support, or an inspiration, or any kind of adjunct to it. If this is not clear from the outset, we shall never make sense of praying.

Mother Mary Clare writes, "prayer is God's activity in us, and not a self-activated process of our own". So the action is God's and the outcome is God's, and the purpose of the relationship which our praying establishes with God is that when we are prepared to be taken out of ourselves and placed by him into the middle of what he is doing, then we receive a part in the result which is his. Father and Son work together and rejoice together, and those who are "in Christ" are given a share in the work and their share in the joy.

Mother Mary Clare continues,

> At the beginning of our learning to pray, therefore, we must
> relate prayer to conversion of life. Prayer, which is the fruit
> of true conversion, is an activity, an adventure, and
> sometimes a dangerous one, since there are occasions
> when it brings neither peace nor comfort, but challenge,
> conflict and new responsibility. This is why so many old
> ways of praying, and books about prayer, seem to let us

down. Too often when we used them we were hoping to get something for ourselves from prayer, perhaps security or a growing sensible realization and knowledge of God. To seek such things in prayer is a mistake. The essential heart of prayer is the throwing away of ourselves in self-oblation to God, so that he can do with us what he wills. Any form of prayer which does not incite a costing giving in love soon becomes sterile, dry and a formal duty.

Mother Mary Clare, *Encountering the Depths*, p. 5

So "reward" will be a better word than "result" when we are exploring this element in praying. Certainly the New Testament has a good deal to say about rewards. We are encouraged to open ourselves to receive the reward of discipleship. For what happens in prayer is that God works through us and in us – he brings in his Kingdom – he heals those in desperate need, in his own time, and in his way of love – he bears their sorrow and pain with them, during the process – and as we saw in the last chapter, he draws us into his peace and joy, not by leaving the world behind but by bringing its horrifying reality into their transfiguring power.

There is a character in Charles Williams's novel *War in Heaven* who "by long practice had accustomed himself in any circumstances – in company, or alone, at work or at rest, in speech or in silence – to withdraw into that place where action is created". He reminds me of another brilliant definition of prayer, that it is "the triumph of action over activity". Our praying should bring us to the same place.

Go tell everyone

Travellers' tales can be as boring as holiday photos and home videos at the wrong time and in the wrong place, and yet both contain a mysterious compulsion. We feel these are experiences which need to be shared. Until they are, they remain incomplete and in some way unfulfilled. The famous Ancient Mariner stopped one of three among the wedding guests, whether they wanted to listen to his tale or not, compelled by the strange desire simply to tell his story. There is a similar compulsion in the Gospel. Christians often sing "we have a gospel to proclaim" – by which they mean good news set on fire by the central fact of Jesus' resurrection. An irreducible aspect of the Easter experience is the desire to tell others about it and, as far as possible, to share it with them.

Dorothy L. Sayers reminded us that the Christian story is never boring (unless it is told badly) and only incomprehensible in the sense that it remains "strange" because people find it searching and demanding. It makes them review their starting points and assumptions, and raises many new and perhaps previously unthought questions. Then, because it is about God, the story is also fascinating – a word which means something that holds us in its own power – by which they mean.

The Easter message is not that Jesus survived death or rose again in his own strength, but that "GOD raised him from the dead", as St Paul repeats over and over again. When the two disciples arrived at Emmaus on the first Easter Day and invited their unknown companion to stay with them for supper (Luke 24.13–35), they recognized Jesus through the breaking of bread and were over-joyed. It opened their eyes not only to Jesus, but also to a new dimension of the power of God. Experiencing that power "they set out that instant and returned to Jerusalem" (Luke 24.33). They couldn't rest until they had at least told their friends who they had seen and what was happening. Those who know the resurrection of Christ through their prayer and praise become apostles – people sent out with a mission and a message. This is another example of prayer in action.

We don't often bring the impulse of mission so close to either Easter or the Eucharist, but the need to tell others of Jesus is built into the experience of knowing his presence with us. Evangelism is not an extra added on to the Easter faith but contained within it, at its heart, and unless that is how we celebrate Easter, we should seriously question its authenticity. An "Easter People" will have Alleluia as their song, as St Augustine preached centuries ago, and they will want God to use them while he teaches the world to sing.

A person who knows the living Lord is diminished unless he or she is an agent of mission. But we need to be clear thinking when we go further and develop strategies for mission. We pray God will use our efforts, though frail and unsatisfactory, to help in his conversion of the world and to bring in his Kingdom. However, it is easy to misconstrue our part in such work. We are fellow-workers, not initiators. If Christians use the word conversion at all, they use it to describe their own con-version, which, as we saw in the last chapter, can be much harder and more costly than we sometimes realize. "Winning souls" is an outworn and unhelpful Christian slogan, because it puts the emphasis in the wrong place – on humanity rather than on God.

We need the humility and the trust to leave the conversion of the world safely in his hands. Our part is to be alert and praying so that we can be used to the full by him in whatever way he wishes.

"I want to preach the Gospel with my life," Charles de Foucauld often said. He was convinced that the most effective method of evangelism for him was to preach the Gospel by living it, and to live it he spent his life in community and in the direct action of prayer. Many people have found this perplexing and wondered what sense it makes. Such confusion is debilitating, because it reveals very painfully how inadequate our prayers have become and how far we are from both God and his world.

Contemplation in the streets

Told in her own words, here is a true-life story of mission and prayer in action.

> A church I used to attend was planning a large-scale mission. Most seemed excited at the prospect of inviting their friends to guest services, "evangelistic supper parties" etc. But I sat back and cringed. Then a friend and I decided to meet regularly to pray together for particular people. We began to do this several months before the "Mission Week" and continued for many months after. It was wonderful the way God answered our prayers and we saw some real changes in individuals and situations.
>
> I did not go to any of the organised activities of the mission, but the fact that it was happening was the original stimulus to our "prayer partnership", and we believed that the hidden work of prayer was the contribution God called us to make at that time.

That woman's discovery about prayer and action is far from unusual. Circumstances in our time are drawing many, or even driving many if you like, towards what has traditionally but misleadingly been called the religious life of which her prayer-partnership was a clear echo.

In our time there is much toing and froing between those who live in Christian communities and those who do not. Carlo Carretto puts it,

Convent walls are becoming thinner and the ceilings ever lower. The laity are becoming conscious of their mission and are searching for a genuine spirituality. It is truly the dawn of a new world to which it would not seem unworthy to give as an aim "contemplation in the streets" and to offer the means of achieving it.

We imagine that in the past living the religious life meant being cut off from the secular world behind closed doors. Dip into some history and you'll see at once that this is simply not how it happened. In the Middle Ages there was a firm and powerful balance between the religious life and secular life. They were both interconnected in a much more dynamic way than we notice. They were two aspects of a single whole, complementary not divided.

In our day with good reason we have been nervous of separating off the sacred from the secular, but so far we have been less successful in reaching a proper balance between them. A division between sacred and secular is impossible, and robs both of their legitimate and creative power which only comes through their complementarity. We have allowed religion to be absorbed by secularism, instead of nourishing the one with the other. This is partly why the Church has been marginalized and become a minority taste. But, at the same time, God is exercising his sovereignty over the whole of life just as he has always done, which is bringing to birth his Kingdom among us and calling us to pray.

The action of praying brings together sacred and secular, though often it will be in hidden ways, which is why we need to know that the heritage of prayer and the vocation to pray is not for the few but for all. More often than not those who are of the Spirit, being used to bring in the Kingdom, nowadays either have little if anything to do with our institutions and tradition or at least sit fairly lightly to them. The wind of the Spirit has always blown its seed to lodge wherever it pleases and many have found this very disturbing, but in our time such disturbance is one way of holding together what should never have been separated.

As we shall see, here is the secret of Taizé. It is a place hidden yet well known, a place which draws people to God from every possible starting point, a place where God calls and commissions and equips, a place where prayer is action, a place where God's Kingdom comes.

"Believe me" said Jesus, "the time approaches, indeed it is already here, when those who are real worshippers will worship the Father in spirit and in truth. Such are the worshippers whom the Father wants" (John 4.23), and it would not be wrong to add that what God wants, he creates and brings into being. He has been converting us all to his Spirit and truth. You could write the history of the Church in our own century (as it must be in any century) as the story of that conversion.

BROTHER ROGER

Every year many thousands of people from every part of the world make the journey to a little village in Burgundy in Eastern France. A few years ago I went the easy way – by car. Brother Roger Schutz who went there to inspect a house, and then bought it and turned it into the famous Taizé community, first went by bicycle. That was in August 1940. He found the village on top of a low ridge of hills which runs parallel to the main road and, like everyone else, to get to it he had a short but rather sharp climb.

Another visitor to Taizé was Father Gerard Hughes who went on foot in 1975 and later described what he found.

> *I climbed the hill to the village. The first impression was that I had walked into a gypsy encampment. The fields on each side of the road were lined with tents, large brown army tents on one side, private tents and caravans on the other and there were hundreds of youngsters wandering about.*
>
> *I wanted to visit Taizé as an unprejudiced, objective observer. I had read about Roger Schutz, a Protestant minister, whose studies in the history of Christianity had convinced him of the need for a revival of the monastic tradition in Protestantism. In 1940 he gathered a group about him, settled in Taizé, where he gave shelter to Jews and other refugees until the Germans took over Vichy, and he had to return to Geneva. In 1944 he returned to Taizé and today (1975) the monastery numbers more than 70 monks, representatives of many Christian denominations of the Reformed, Orthodox and Roman Catholic Churches. The Rule of Taizé is a masterpiece of simplicity and fidelity to the gospel, and Roger Schutz' Letters from Taizé are marked by that same simplicity. His message is that Christ calls all men, irrespective of race, creed or social status and calls us all into his unity and peace.*

Each visitor or pilgrim to Taizé notices something particular which he or she takes to be special. Two things struck me when I went, not really knowing what to expect: peace and personal space.

There were many thousands camping in Taizé at the time, mostly young; and while I was there, a good many families from Eastern Europe were also present, enjoying a real holiday together for the first time after the opening of the borders between East and West. Inevitably there was tremendous noise and activity. Thousands living together could hardly be silent as they went about their daily chores. And yet it was not an unbearable din, which it might have been. Instead of a hubbub, there was a deep and unshakeable peace within everything that was going on – the children's games, the groups of young people singing, dancing, entertaining themselves, the queues for meals, the parties relaxing together in the sunshine.

Then, when the bells rang for worship, the whole population crowded into the famous Church of Reconciliation and really did keep silence. Again there were thousands present and yet, in spite of the press, somehow there seemed to be a rich and satisfying space around each person. No one felt crowded or pushed about. In that vast Christian assembly there was room for everyone to be themselves before God, and there was time and freedom for each person to express their own individual longing for him in any way they wished.

In many ways, although the story of Taizé and its development is well documented, it remains one of the world's hidden secrets. Remote in so many ways, devoted to the daily round and common task, who would have thought this Christian community could have such a powerful influence on contemporary life? But that is how it is, reminding us that often mission takes place at home long before it can go abroad. To be a missionary is to be a faithful witness to God wherever he happens to have placed us.

Key turning points at Taizé came in 1949 when the first seven brothers made their commitment to community life, and in 1974 when the brothers decided to have a worldwide council of youth. At the beginning, Brother Roger cared for children, refugees, and the elderly. Then, after over twenty years of community life with a special emphasis on ecumenism, rather reluctantly at first, the brothers decided to concentrate their work among young people seeking Christ. Brother Roger wrote in his diary, "I wonder if we shall have the strength to go ahead in a commitment with the young people. I should like to give up the idea of a council of youth". Yet the work did go ahead and it is this particular ministry which flourishes and makes Taizé such a magnet.

Father Gerard Hughes suggests why,

> *Why are most of [the churches] falling down and empty, apart*
> *from a few elderly faithful, while Taizé, situated in a remote*
> *part of France, cannot accommodate its numbers, especially*
> *the young? The answer, I think, lies in the simplicity of Taizé.*
> *God loves and welcomes all men, coerces none. The monks*
> *believe this and become in St Paul's words, "the goodness of*
> *God". When this goodness is manifest, it attracts. Taizé is a*
> *living proof of this truth. I have attended many meetings on*
> *pastoral work when the same wrong questions are asked:*
> *"Why are so few people interested in religion any more and*
> *have given up church-going?" It is a false question, because*
> *people are interested in religion, but not in the kind of religion*
> *which does not touch our deeper longings. The false question*
> *inevitably produces the same monotonous false answer: "It*
> *is because of the materialism and permissiveness of our*
> *twentieth century and the general deterioration in moral*
> *standards"; a comfortable answer for the clergy because it*
> *demands nothing from us except moral disapproval at which*
> *we excel. A truer answer to the question "Why do people no*
> *longer come to Church?" is "Because they can no longer*
> *recognise in it the breadth of Christ's love." When they do see*
> *it, they flock in, as at Taizé.*

When anyone attends worship at Taizé there is a special
atmosphere which includes much more than the haunting music
that has become popular all over the world.

> *Many feel – and feel increasingly – that they are not so*
> *much making an effort as somehow responding to a*
> *mysterious reality beyond their grasp, responding to God.*
> *They sense that this suits their human nature – that they*
> *were made for this. As you leave the church, you sense that*
> *you must somehow continue to live what you have done.*
> *This is, as Christians would say, worship in the Spirit.*

The ecumenical commitment continues too, of course, and is now
large enough to involve not only all Christian people, but all people
of faith, and indeed all people who are seeking faith and willing to give of themselves in its pursuit. "Most people", says
Brother Roger, "love Taizé for its open doors and for the way it
enters into dialogue with so many".

Deeper still, another factor on which the community's work of mission is built is a particular insight into the nature of religious commitment, especially for those living in community.

> *In the Rule of Taizé, the brothers prefer to use the word "engagement" rather than "vow". This is no matter of mere linguistics, but a change of emphasis from the context of legal obligation to that of voluntary commitment; from the part of man to that of God. The traditional term "vow" and the traditional form in which it is taken by monks and nuns underlines the commitment of the person, his responsibility and by implication the awful penalties of failure. Taizé seeks however to change this by emphasising the response made to the call of God in whom the individual may trust to lead him further.*

Peter Moore, *Tomorrow is too Late*, p. 18

Brother Roger has written in the Rule,

> *If this rule were ever to be regarded as an end in itself and to dispense us from always seeking more and more to discover God's design, the love of Christ and the light of the Holy Spirit, we would be imposing on ourselves a useless burden. Then it would be better never to have written it.*

Then, when the brothers at Taizé took a deliberate decision to concentrate their work among the young, they invited them not to take vows or to make promises but to become engaged to a commitment to what they called "a pilgrimage of trust on earth".

> *The "pilgrimage of trust on earth" animated by Taizé for years now does not organise young people into a movement centred on Taizé but stimulates them to become creators of peace, bearers of trust, in their towns and villages, in their parishes, with all the generations, from children to the elderly. Everyone can turn their life into a pilgrimage of trust... by praying... by trying to understand those who are far away because of their backgrounds, their choices... by undertaking gestures of reconciliation in one's own situation... by communicating to others a fine human hope.*

ANDREW

Andrew was Simon Peter's brother. He is not often in the limelight
in the accounts of Jesus and the disciples. Much of the part he
played remains hidden. Yet he brought Peter to Jesus in the first
place, which is the origin of the tradition that Andrew is the first
and greatest missionary. Perhaps it is significant that we know
hardly anything of what Andrew said, and yet we can plainly see
the results of his life of praying and being with Jesus. From other
information in the New Testament, mainly about Peter, we know
the name of Andrew's father – Jona (John 21.15), and that he had a
sister-in-law (Mark 1.30). The family lived in Bethsaida in Galilee
(John 1.44), which was also the home town of Philip.

We might call Andrew "the fourth man" among Jesus' disciples,
although he was probably the first of the twelve actually to see and
to hear Jesus. It was Peter, James, and John who formed the inner
circle, closest to Jesus. They shared the most intimate and powerful
moments of his ministry. Jesus took them with him, but not
Andrew, when:

- he healed Jairus' daughter (an insight for them into Jesus'
  vocation to bring new life out of death);

- he went to the Mount of the Transfiguration (a vision of Jesus'
  resurrection and glory);

- he went to Gethsemane (where he faced the full extent and
  horror of the total cost which the bringing in of his Father's
  Kingdom would require of him).

According to the Fourth Gospel, which almost certainly contains
some historical details of the life of Jesus from a very early source
which is accurate and reliable, Andrew began as a disciple of John
the Baptist. He was present when John pointed to Jesus as *Messiah*.

*The next day again John was standing with two of his
disciples; and he looked at Jesus as he walked, and said,
"Behold, the Lamb of God!" The two disciples heard him
say this, and they followed Jesus. Jesus turned, and saw
them following, and said to them, "What do you seek?"
And they said to him, "Rabbi (which means Teacher),
where are you staying?" He said to them, "Come and see".
They came and saw where he was staying; and they stayed
with him that day, for it was about the tenth hour. One of
the two who heard John speak and followed him, was*

*Andrew, Simon Peter's brother. And he first found his
brother Simon, and said to him, "We have found the
Messiah" (which means Christ).*

John 1.35–42a

Some time later – exactly how long we do not know – Jesus saw
Andrew and Peter at work, fishing, and he started them on their life
of discipleship.

*Passing along by the Sea of Galilee, he saw Simon and
Andrew the brother of Simon casting a net in the sea; for
they were fishermen. And Jesus said to them, "Follow me
and I will make you fishers of men". And immediately they
left their nets and followed him.*

Mark 1.16–17

Andrew's role as a disciple may have been quite well defined
rather than fortuitous. He was the one who enabled others,
even among the twelve, "to be with Jesus". At any rate that is
what happened on at least two occasions recorded in the
New Testament.

*Jesus said to Philip, "how are we to buy bread, so that
these people may eat?" This he said to test him, for he
himself knew what he would do. Philip answered him,
"Two hundred denarii would not buy enough bread for
each of them to get a little." One of his disciples, Andrew,
Simon Peter's brother, said to him, "there is a lad here
who has five barley loaves and two small fish; but what
are they among so many?" Jesus said, "Make the people
sit down".*

John 6.1–10

*Now among those who went up to worship at the feast were
some Greeks. So these first came to Philip, who was from
Bethsaida in Galilee, and said to him, "Sir, we wish to see
Jesus." Philip went and told Andrew; Andrew went with
Philip and told Jesus. And Jesus answered them, "The hour
has come for the Son of man to be glorified. Truly, truly, I
say to you, unless a grain of wheat falls into the earth
and dies, it remains alone; but if it dies, it bears much
fruit. He who loves his life loses it, and he who hates his
life in this world will keep it for eternal life. If any one*

*serves me, he must follow me; and where I am, there shall
my servant be also; if any one serves me the Father will
honour him".*

John 12.20–26

Although we have noted how Andrew was left out of several
special events in Jesus' ministry, he was with the inner circle at one
key moment just before Jesus' arrest and trial.

*As Jesus sat on the Mount of Olives opposite the temple,
Peter and James and John and Andrew asked him
privately, "Tell us when will this be, and what will be the
sign when these things are all to be accomplished?" And
Jesus began to say to them, "Take heed that no one leads
you astray. Many will come in my name saying, 'I am he!'
and they will lead many astray. And when you hear of wars
and rumours of wars, do not be alarmed; this must take
place, but the end is not yet. For nation will rise against
nation, and kingdom against kingdom; there will be
earthquakes in various places, there will be famines; this is
but the beginnings of the sufferings."*

Mark 13.3–8

Before his death Jesus needed to teach his friends about the
relationship between mission and self-giving, between losing in
order to find and the true cost of following him. Significantly in the
New Testament, the word martyr occurs more frequently than
the word witness, and the words are in several cases inter- change-
able. The one is inextricably linked with the other. To be a witness,
to be a person with a mission, inevitably entails a willingness to
give without counting the cost in terms of personal suffering, often
as we know (and not only in New Testament times either) of
persecution and death.

The last reference to Andrew in the Bible comes after the
resurrection, when the disciples and those who knew Jesus returned
to Jerusalem, and stayed there waiting for the gift of the
Holy Spirit.

*Then they returned to Jerusalem from the mount called
Olivet, which is near Jerusalem, a sabbath's day's journey
away; and when they had entered, they went up to the
upper room, where they were staying, Peter and John and
James and Andrew, Philip and Thomas, Bartholomew and*

*Matthew, James the son of Alphaeus and Simon the Zealot
and Judas the son of James. All these with one accord
devoted themselves to prayer, together with the women and
Mary the mother of Jesus, and with his brothers.*

Acts 1.12–14

According to the early Christian historian Eusebius, Andrew then
went on to preach in Scythia, an area near the Black Sea which was
believed at the time to be on the edge of the world where civilization and barbarism met. Other writers mention him as evangelizing
in Epirus in Macedonia and in Achaia, what we call mainland
Greece. These traditions may be acceptable, but less so is the claim
that he reached Byzantium.

He is said to have been crucified at Patras, in Achaia, being first
scourged and then bound to a diagonal cross in order that his
suffering might be prolonged. The traditional story, which is
almost certainly a piece of hagiography and rather unreliable,
relates how Andrew preached from the cross to twenty-two
thousand people, and lingered for two days before he died. His
hearers felt, "this bold and debonair man ought not to suffer thus",
and many were converted.

READINGS

1. Living on the streets

*Our vocation is contemplation in the streets. For me this is
quite costly. The desire to continue living here in the
Sahara for ever is so strong that I am already suffering in
anticipation of the order that will certainly come from my
superiors: "Brother Charles, leave for Marseilles, leave for
Morocco, leave for Venezuela, leave for Detroit.*

*You must go back among men, mix with them. Live your
intimacy with God in the noise of their cities. It will be
difficult but you must do it. And for this the grace of God
will not fail you. Every morning, after Mass and
meditation, you will make your way to work in a store or
shipyard. And when you get back in the evening, tired like
all poor men forced to earn their living, you will enter the
little chapel of the brotherhood and remain for a long time
in adoration; bringing to your prayers all that world of*

suffering, of darkness, and often of sin, in the midst of which you have lived for eight hours taking your share of pain and toil."

Carlo Carretto, *Letters from the Desert*

2. Bringing others to Christ

Bishop Azariah, the famous missionary bishop in India, insisted every Christian should be an evangelist. Once he asked a large congress of Christians how many people they had brought to Christ since their baptism? One old woman struggled to her feet with difficulty and said with sorrow, "I have only brought five people to Christ since I was baptised." She knew five was few, but for some, perhaps five would be many.

3. Inward and outward

One intense conviction: any communication with God leads us towards our neighbour. The sign which proves the authenticity of our inner life – of our relationship with Jesus Christ – is how attentive we are to others. If our neighbours vanish from our dialogue with Christ, then our love for God has more to do with some mythical deity completely detached from human concerns than with the Christ of the Gospel.

Brother Roger

4. For their sakes, I consecrate myself

In any lifetime there are innumerable little deaths – always painful and frightening – changing house, seeing a child go away from home for the first time, losing one's job, leaving one's homeland, the break-up of a marriage, retirement – you can think of many more. There are also for every woman and man occasions when a dying for others is required – one's own cherished plan surrendered so that someone else may have a more important breakthrough; one's work used and credit given to someone who may need it more; one's lifestyle curtailed by another's demand upon us; one's security sacrificed so that others may be helped. It hardly ever happens with any heroics or romance. It is hard and unacknowledged.

John V. Taylor, *Weep Not for Me*, pp. 42–43

5. *If you love one another, all shall know you are my disciples*

Unlike most traditional monastic rules, the Rule of Taizé was inspired by an experiment in community living which had already been going on for some years: a number of brothers had already been living its chief principles for some time. The Rule does not lay down the hours of prayer or details of this kind, nor does it tell the brothers what they should wear. Instead it attempts to suggest a spirit and to motivate and inspire a way of life. It often does this by quoting phrases from the Bible; this may be taken as an illustration of the fact that the first brothers were well grounded in Scripture. "There is a danger in having indicated with this rule only the essentials for a common life", says the Rule. "Better to run that risk, and not settle into complacency and routine... That Christ may grow in me, I must know my own weakness and that of my brothers. For them I will become all things to all, and even give my life, for Christ's sake and the Gospel's."

Brother Roger, *Taizé Rule*

6. *The missionary task*

There is a story told of P. T. Forsyth, when he was principal of Hackney College, London, where candidates were trained for the ministry. A man of great earnestness visited the college and expressed the hope that the salvation of souls was its main business. In a flash Forsyth replied, "Our chief concern here is not with souls but with the Gospel". The proper missionary task is to tell the story of God's love and the power of life over death, which Jesus' resurrection (and much else) demonstrates.

7. Continuing to the end

*Perhaps one of the most basic and important things we can
learn – or rather be reminded of – is the need of spiritual
masters. This is perhaps one of our greatest lacks in this
splendid hour of grace-filled renewal. We have all too few
spiritual masters to lead us, guide us, spur us on to full
Christian realisation. It is what so many are seeking today,
a true master, one who has been there and can show us the
way, one in whom we can place our confidence. So few
have been willing to pay the price, really to die and rise
again in Christ, to come to that fullness of Christian
maturation that can engender life.*

Basil Pennington, *Monastic Exchange*,
vol. IV, no. 3, Autumn 1972

8. That you may have life

*something given
And taken, in a lifetime's death in love,
Ardour and selflessness and self-surrender.
For most of us, there is only the unattended
Moment, the moment in and out of time,
The distraction fit, lost in a shaft of sunlight,
The wild thyme unseen, or the winter lightning
Or the waterfall, or music heard so deeply
That it is not heard at all, but you are the music
While the music lasts. These are only hints and guesses,
Hints followed by guesses; and the rest
Is prayer, observance, discipline, thought and action.
The hint half guessed, the gift half understood, is Incarnation.
Here the impossible union
Of spheres of existence is actual,
Here the past and future
Are conquered and reconciled.*

T. S. Eliot, *Four Quartets*

PRAYERS

1. Adoration

*The right question may be not: "What good does
prayer do?" but "What good does the praying
Christian do?" The praying Christian is one whose
prayer is part of a converse with God which includes
actions and orientations as well as words. Through
the centuries, despite the failures and the scandals,
the impact of Christianity in creating not a few
Christ-like lives has been through Christians for
whom prayer has been an integral part of their
sharing in the divine love.*

Michael Ramsey, *Be Still and Know*

Again, begin by asking God to fill you with love and
praise, and then go on and allow him to lead you
forward into loving action "and do all such good
works as he has prepared for us" to do.

2. Penitence

*The ministry of reconciliation is part of the life of a
reconciled and reconciling Church. This means a
Church aware that it owes its own existence to the
reconciliation of the Cross, and has a worship ever
deepened by that awareness. It means also a
Church which prays for the world with the question
"Who is my neighbour?" ceaselessly in heart and
mind and outgoing action.*

Michael Ramsey, *Be Still and Know*

Think of the greatness of the forgiveness you have
received and contrast it with the smallness of the
forgiveness you too often offer. Pray Jesus' prayer,
"Forgive us our sins as we forgive those who sin
against us".

3.   Intercession

The Church is called to be a community which speaks to the world in God's name and speaks to God from the middle of the world's darkness and frustration. The prayer with beautiful buildings and lovely music must be a prayer which also speaks from the places where men and women work, or lack work, and are sad and hungry, suffer and die.

Michael Ramsey, *Be Still and Know*

Ask God to show you what work for his kingdom he wants you to do for the sake of either others you know or one specific person known to you.

4.   Dedication

The outcome of time spent in prayer will be determinded not only by our designs but by God's act in shaping both the time and ourselves. To pray thus is to expose one's own weakness in God's presence and to ask him to use our little fragments of wanting and loving beyond what we ask or have. If the enthusiasm of a full heart brings us near to God, no less near to him is the prayer of a frail and sincere wanting. It will open the soul to a new pouring in of the love of God.

Michael Ramsey, *Be Still and Know*

Stand with God as well as before him, and see how his presence and work are within you. In Jesus, he promises to be with us until the end of time, and so make the response and offer him your intention to be with him always.

5. *Written Prayers*

Teach us, good Lord, to serve thee as thou deservest:
  to give, and not to count the cost;
  to fight and not to heed the wounds;
  to toil, and not to seek for rest;
  to labour, and not to ask for any reward save that of
    knowing that we do thy will;
through Jesus Christ our Lord. Amen

St Ignatius Loyola, 1495–1556

O Lord Jesus Christ, you have commanded us to make known the good news of your love to all nations: help us so to experience your forgiveness, grace and peace that we may want all other people to share those blessings and to come into the family of the one Father, to whom be all gratitude, love and praise for ever and ever. Amen

New Every Morning

BIBLIOGRAPHY

A. M. Allchin, *The Dynamic of Tradition*, Darton, Longman and Todd, 1981 *A Taste of Liberty*, SLG Press, Oxford, 1982

Christopher Bryant, *The Heart in Pilgrimage*, Darton, Longman and Todd, 1980

Carlo Carretto, *Letters from the Desert*, Darton, Longman and Todd, 1972

A Carthusian, *The Way of Silent Love*, Darton, Longman and Todd, 1993

P. Franklin Chambers, *A Little Book of Baron von Hügel*, Geoffrey Bles, 1945

David Coomes, *A Careless Rage for Life*, Lion Publishing, 1992

Catherine de Hueck Doherty, *Poustinia*, Collins, 1975

T. S. Eliot, *Complete Poems and Plays*, Faber and Faber, 1969

Patrick Leigh Fermor, *A Time of Gifts*, Penguin Books, 1977

Robert Gittings, *Young Thomas Hardy*, Penguin Books, 1978

Caroline Glyn, "Caedmon", published in *Christian*, 1975, vol. 2, no. 4

Dag Hammarskjöld, *Markings*, Faber and Faber, 1964

Rosemary Hartill, *Were you There?*, SPCK, London, 1995

Deborah Duncan Honorè (ed.), *Trevor Huddleston, Essays on his life and work*, Oxford University Press, 1988

Trevor Huddleston, *Naught for your Comfort*, Collins, 1956

Gerard Hughes, *In Search of a Way*, Darton, Longman and Todd, 1986

Eric James, *Judge Not*, Christian Action, 1989

Julian of Norwich, translated by Clifton Wolters, *Revelations of Divine Love*, Penguin Books, 1966

D. H. Lawrence, "Only man", from *Let there be God*, an anthology, Religious Education Press Ltd, Oxford, 1968

C. S. Lewis, *Poems*, edited by Walter Hooper, Geoffrey Bles, 1964 *Reflections on the Psalms*, Geoffrey Bles, 1958

Thomas Merton, *The Wisdom of the Desert*, Sheldon Press, 1961

Peter Moore, *Tomorrow is Too Late*, A. R. Mowbray, 1970

Geoffrey Moorhouse, *The Fearful Void*, Penguin Books, 1986

Mother Mary Clare, *Encountering the Depths*, SLG Press, Oxford, 1973

Malcolm Muggeridge, *Something Beautiful for God*, Fontana Books, 1972

Werner Pelz, *Crowning Absurdity*, Talks for the BBC

Gerald Priestland, *The Unquiet Staircase*, Grafton Books, 1988

Robert Runcie, *One Light for One World*, SPCK, London, 1988

Dorothy L. Sayers, *The Man Born to be King*, Victor Gollancz Ltd, 1943

E. K. Talbot, *Retreat Addresses*, SPCK, London, 1954

John V. Taylor, *Weep Not for Me*, World Council of Churches, Geneva, 1986

William Temple, *Christian Faith and Life*, SCM Press Ltd, 1957

R. S. Thomas, *Frequencies*, Macmillan London Ltd, 1978

Evelyn Underhill, *The Mount of Purification*, Longmans, Green and Co., 1960

A. R. Vidler (ed.), *Soundings*, Cambridge University Press, 1962

Herbert Waddams, *Life and Fire of Love*, SPCK, London, 1964

Simone Weil, *Waiting on God*, Routledge and Kegan Paul Ltd, 1951

H. A. Williams, *The True Wilderness*, Constable and Co. Ltd, 1965